# coloring outside the lines

## a punk rock memoir

by
Aimee Cooper

Rowdy's Press
Texas     uh, that's it

Rowdy's Press
P.O. Box 847
Elgin, Texas 78621

Printed in USA
Second Edition
    Second Printing, 2003
ISBN 0-97231171-8
Cover Design: Christia Madacsi

Grateful acknowledgement is made for
permission to reprint The L.A. Weekly cover
by Mark Vallen

The author can be contacted at possumwp@aol.com

Thanks go to the following people:  my amazing editor, Maggie Ehrig; my parents, for their love and support; my veterinarian Kellee and my brother Jon, for their great comments and correction of my questionable grammar; Christia, who did a fantastic job designing the cover; DeeDee at Expressions in Film and Video, for all her help; my aunt Carlene, for her encouragement; Samantha, for her wonderful suggestions; the neat folks at Postnet, in Austin; everybody at AlphaGraphics; Bridget, for the generous donation of her feet; my friends Mel, Brenda, Amber, and Kay, for continuing to reassure me that yes, they liked it!; all my pets, for patiently waiting for their food and walks while I finished that 'one paragraph'; my beloved dog Clancy; Malissa, Maggie, Emil, Mark, and the rest of the TC, for sharing an incredible adventure with me; Bobbi Brat, for her courage and her friendship; and to Michelle Burns, who taught me that if you think you can't do something, you very well may be right. But on the other hand, maybe you can...

<u>Dedicated to</u>

Sue

For always being by my side,
even when you aren't.


I did it, Sue!

# 1

It was a perfect California day.

I was laying on my back in a large field, waiting for the music to begin. There was an azure sky above me, with barely a hint of clouds. The blades of grass felt nice against the backs of my legs, and I was filled with a wonderful mixture of anticipation and warm contentment. Mick Jagger. I was finally going to get to see Mick Jagger.

I'd been hoping to see him ever since I got my first hormone. The wild singer for the Stones had come to represent everything I was looking for. He was adventure. No, he was... *danger.* It was a long way from my East Coast upbringing to this field in southern California, and it would take every one of those three thousand miles to allow me to embrace my rebellious side. But as the opening, forgettable act gave way to a second, and then a third, my excitement began to ebb. It's awfully hard to work yourself up into a rock and roll frenzy, when the idea of an afternoon cat nap has become so enticing.

Finally, and at long last, it was time. They were here. *He* was here. The band climbed onto the stage as I jumped to my feet. My God, here we go... And then a funny thing happened. An imposter took the stage.

Before me stood a small, skinny man, wearing a red plastic

jumpsuit, with a little matching red plastic cap. He pranced about, pointing at the audience, while his band played obediently behind him. I shook my head. This couldn't be Jagger! It just couldn't. This guy wasn't danger. He was... he was... silly.

The sun felt hot. The red jumpsuit was hurting my eyes. And there were still no clouds in the sky.

# 2

Six years. That was what junior high and high school in New York were for me - a tunnel that wound on and on for six years, with only the vague promise of an exit.

For some girls high school is a glorious experience. I wasn't one of those girls. While most of my friends blossomed as teenagers, I found myself more daffodil than orchid. Being alone thus became a natural state of affairs for me; I filled the vacuum created by my unpopularity with pets and books and a lot of self-administered pep talks, all geared to assure me that it would get better. I mean, it had to get better, didn't it?

As I turned seventeen, however, what had been labeled solitude took a hard tack towards isolation, and a constant, dull unhappiness. I wanted to have an adventure. I wanted... I needed... to have fun. So when that college brochure showed up at my door, the one with the photo of coeds riding horses on the Santa Barbara coast, I was already packed.

College academics at the University of California was an oxymoron, at least for me. That freshman year there was no academics. There was skateboarding and hitchhiking and surfing. The few times that a book was cracked, it was done on the beach; I would return home with sand between the pages and a newly sunburned face, but with no more knowledge than when I left. It was wonderful.

Eventually my first year of college came to an end, and I made the reluctant journey back to New York. It was shaping up to be a long three months, waiting for the return of fall...

I was laying on my bed, browsing through a teen magazine, when an article caught my eye. The headline read 'No Date? Why Wait!' No date? That was me, all right.

The gist of the story was that a young woman should not be sitting around waiting for a boy to ask her out - it was up to the girl to empower herself by making the first move. In 1977 this was something I had never heard of - well, outside of the annual Sadie Hawkins dances. But as I read the article I thought to myself - they're right. They're absolutely right. Why shouldn't I ask him out? I mean, the instructions are right here (flipping to page 147). I can definitely do this. All that was needed now was to find the 'him'.

That problem was solved the next day, during my visit to the city. He had gotten himself lost, and needed directions; his eyes were light blue, and he had wavy hair that played hide and seek with his shirt collar. Actually, I was just as puzzled as he was, but I didn't tell him that. Instead, I stood close to him as we poured over his map, flirted a little (page 148), and then did it. I asked him out. And you know what? He said yes!

The next weekend I took the train back into New York City, and hailed a cab for the Museum of Natural History. We chose that as our starting point, before going on to Central Park. I dashed up the steps two at a time until I reached the high landing, and looked about me. But my date wasn't there.

I waited. Half an hour. Forty minutes. Fifty four minutes. After another half an hour I finally had to admit to myself that it was no use; he just wasn't coming. My lips tried to tremble but I determinedly turned them back into a smile. Okay. Okay. This wasn't so bad. As a matter of fact, it was better this way. I now had the whole day on my hands, and a whole city to fill it with.

First I phoned my father; he was always there for me when I needed reassurance, or comfort. After Dad told me in no uncertain terms what an idiot the boy was, I felt much better. And instead of my taking the train back, he offered to pick me up later.

Question was, which way to go? I looked north, then south, and smiled. Greenwich Village. The Village was always lots of fun. It had unusual shops, and even more unusual people. It was fun to just let yourself get lost, and that's what I did.

Meandering down the winding streets and past cluttered shops, I came upon a small club called The Village Gate. The faded notice on the door announced that Johnny Thunders and the Heartbreakers would be playing there that evening. Johnny... who? I peered closer at the black and white flyer, but it wasn't much help. Other than time and place, it provided me with no further clues to Johnny Thunders. Even now I wonder what led me to step through that doorway.

After calling my dad on a nearby payphone to tell him where he could find me, I paid for my ticket, and went inside.

The club was quite small, with curiously low ceilings and a paucity of tables and chairs. The tables that were there ringed a tiny, floor-level stage, in the shape of a half-moon. The room was intimate, and strange, and - dark! I'd never seen so much black leather in one room before. Leather jackets were everywhere, along with spiked haircuts, all sticky and elongated. Despite the unusual look of the clientele, I judged myself to be the youngest person in there.

I sat down at a table next to the stage and ordered a ginger ale. As the waiter brought me my drink he seemed a bit amused; I gathered that soda pop was not a popular request.

The ginger ale clasped tightly in my hand, I waited for the show to begin, all the while casting furtive glances at my fellow audience members. Suddenly the only remaining light went out, and Johnny Thunders and the Heartbreakers took the stage.

Johnny was just a couple of feet from me; of average height and nondescript looks, he hardly made an overpowering first impression. But when he grabbed the mike and the first note was hit, everything that had been missing that day under the warm California sun exploded onto the tiny, dingy stage. His music was raw, and wild, and powerful. It was what I had been searching for.

By the time my father arrived to pick me up, I felt completely at home; I waved to him as he made his way, horrified, through the smoky room.

"Hi Dad!" I called cheerfully.

It is a measure of my father's goodness and understanding that he let me live. On the drive home I chattered like a blue jay about the band and the music and the people I had seen.

It had begun.

# 3

I returned to school the month after seeing Johnny Thunders, determined to find out as much as I could about punk rock.

My attempts to learn more, however, were frustrated by the lack of information available; while there were plenty of articles about the Sex Pistols and the Boomtown Rats and the Clash, these were English bands, reflecting on an English culture. As far as the New York punk scene went, it was already growing stagnant. Popular bands like The Talking Heads and The Ramones added musical sophistication, or humor, but that was the last thing I wanted.

The answer came almost by accident, in a worn newspaper left discarded in a local record store. It was called Slash.

Created by Steve Samiof and Claude Bessy, aka 'Kickboy', and edited by Bob Biggs, Slash reported on the Los Angeles punk rock scene. This was a surprise in itself - I didn't even know that there were punk bands in Los Angeles. It was a large magazine, with a mixture of professional type and handwritten ads, and printed on the kind of soft paper that is guaranteed to yellow with age. There were about thirty pages in the copy I found, well worth its price of fifty cents. Slash's articles weren't just dry descriptions of groups and songs and the latest scenemakers; they were stories of adventures - adventures that had already occurred, and those yet to come.

Finding copies of Slash wasn't easy - only a couple of record stores carried the magazine, and they did so with a discouraging apathy. I, on the other hand, devoured every page of every issue I could scavenge, memorizing the bands that Kickboy wrote about. Even their names said so much - The Germs, The Circle Jerks, Vicious Circle, Black Flag, X. I knew one thing without anyone even telling me - when these bands played, there were no matching red caps.

The punk gigs took place in small, established venues like the Whiskey on Sunset Boulevard and the Starwood on Santa Monica Boulevard, but they also used some of the lodges belonging to local community service groups. It was one of those smaller halls that became the setting for an attack - one that not only shook the punk community, but changed the course of my future, as well.

Kickboy recounted the story with forceful prose and disturbing photos. It took place at an Elk's Lodge, in Hollywood. Several local bands had been booked, and the concert was noisy and boisterous; despite the high energy level, however, it was a relatively peaceful concert. But not for long.

Without warning the Los Angeles police raided the club, and the hall exploded in a violent outbreak of beatings and arrests. As the kids poured outside, they shouted in anger and disbelief at the unprovoked attack. I read their stories, transfixed - then my eyes moved to the accompanying photo on the next page.

The picture was of a young girl; she was wide-eyed, frightened, with blood running down her face from a deep cut in her hair. But there was something else in her eyes, something beyond the palpable fear: resolve. Her love for punk rock was not going to be stopped by the swing of a billy club. She would defiantly come back, whether the next day or the next week, to the Whisky or the Starwood or the VFW hall on the corner. And there was one more thing that I knew.

I was going to be there, too.

# 4

I was still winding down my college career, finishing off classes and fulfilling my credits, but by then my thoughts and my energy were elsewhere. Ninety-two miles away, to be exact. Due south.

I would scan the ads in the smaller Los Angeles newspapers for punk rock gigs, then I would take off early, or cut class altogether, and head down to Hollywood. Until I could become part of that strange and tumultuous scene, I wanted to visit it as often as possible. Usually it was the bands that were the most memorable; other times, it was the less tangible discoveries that flooded my senses, like visions of bizarre dancing, or the sounds of bottles breaking and boots scraping the pavement. Not this night, though; this night belonged to one girl.

It was a smallish hall in a rundown part of town, and the band drew few people that night. There were some kids dancing, but more of them were standing around, watching, waiting. At the edge of the dance pit stood a girl. I never saw her face, for her back was towards me; her hair, though, was memorable, both for its beauty and its oddity.

Its beauty was obvious; long and straight and silky, it reached all the way to the small of her back. What was odd was that this was a punk concert, and there were rules about that; they may have been unspoken rules, but they were there, as firmly planted as the stars' handprints on Hollywood Boulevard.

Punk rock meant short hair.

Both heavy metal and hippie music, once the bastion of rebels and now of the lackeys of the music establishment, were represented by long hair. Punk rockers went in the opposite direction, and it cost them. In the real world, short, spiked hair or a shaved head were considered by some to be an invitation to a beating, or at the very least, unrelenting verbal abuse. To punks, it was the price they paid for being different, and they were willing to pay that price. Out *there*. In here, inside the clubs, it was their turf. You either became one of them, or you stayed the hell out.

A word had cropped up for those who tried to be weekend warriors, or who were only slumming through this isolated world - they were called posers, and it was just about the worst insult that could be hurled at a punk. Maybe the girl with the long hair didn't know all this; she probably just wandered in, curious about the odd clothes and hair. But it didn't take too long for her lesson to begin.

Out of the corner of my vision came a gremlin-like creature. She was short, with jet black hair, pale white skin, and an unexplained anger that tore through her features. She slipped behind the girl, and before I realized what was going to happen, she pulled out a lighter and set that long, silky hair on fire. I should have moved, or called out a warning, but I was too stunned to react. The same could not be said for the girl. Spinning around quickly, she stamped the flame out with her hands, then looked around fearfully. She may not have understood the message fully, but she got the gist of it.

*You don't belong here.*

Her fear turned to anger and then, as common sense took hold, to resignation. She grabbed her purse, and ran to the exit.

I scanned the room, but the gremlin had disappeared into the darkness. My hand went unconsciously to my own shoulder-length hair, as I wondered when I would see her again.

# 5

Not all of the gigs I went to were punk. There was a young, popular British band called The Jam, and they were coming to Los Angeles; their songs were lighthearted, with a lively beat, and the members of the trio looked a bit like the young Beatles. It would prove to be an unforgettable concert... but not because of the music.

It was early when I got to the hall and the band was still rehearsing, but for some reason they allowed me in anyway. I strolled around the empty floor, elated to be there, but trying to look cool and nonchalant as well. After their practice set, the three members of The Jam left the stage. I assumed that would be as close as I got to them - until one of the roadies called to me. He knelt down on the stage and in a friendly voice asked if I wanted to go backstage and meet the band. Did I want to meet the band?! My face gave him his answer. Oh well, nonchalance was overrated anyway.

The three young men were hanging around a small room. It reminded me a little of the classrooms where high school band practice was held; there were a few plastic chairs scattered about, and instruments lay propped against the wall. I turned to get instructions from my roadie friend, but he had disappeared. I was on my own.

One of the band members looked up at me, and gave me a

quick, welcoming nod before turning back to his guitar. I shyly walked over to one of the chairs and slid down onto it. It was so quiet in the room; there were no sounds other than the absent-minded strumming of a guitar... well, except for one. It was the kind of noise that makes you feel like you've just come out of a barber shop - you know, when you realize that there are still some hairs stuck under your shirt. Prickly. Irritating.

The source of the sound was a young girl standing on the other side of the room. Her hair was bleached blonde, while heavy gel made it stand up in spikes. She wore black eye liner and a short black skirt, which only served to accentuate her pudgy thighs. In a strange way, the black liner and the too short skirt made her look even younger than her years, an illusion that I doubt she was trying to achieve. She looked to be about seven-teen.

After a fleeting glance at me, she turned all her attention back to the Jam member. With one arm slung over his shoulder, she grilled the musician non-stop, in that high, whiny voice. Where were they from? Were they really from England? Where were they staying? The questioning went on and on. She did everything but shine a light in the poor boy's face. He patiently withstood the interrogation, though his interest in her seemed perfunctory. She was determined, however, and when they finally left together, she had a look of triumph. He had a look of boredom.

One of the remaining musicians noticed me. He was slightly built, with short, tidy dark hair and a boyish face. He looked me up and down, evaluating my probable character; whatever he saw appeared to satisfy him.

"Excuse me, love, would you do me a favor?" I nodded word-lessly. "Would you watch my guitar for me? Make sure no one steals it?"

I again nodded. He placed the instrument against the chair next to me, and left the room. Now it was just me and the guitar; I felt a little silly, as there was no one for me to guard it against, but

I dutifully stood my post.

Eventually the band returned, and I was relieved of my position. The concert proved to be noneventful, but fun. When the last note had played and the lights came up, I prepared to leave. It was getting pretty late by that time and the drive up to Santa Barbara still lay ahead of me. Some motion on the stage caught my attention; it was the same roadie who had let me backstage. He signalled for me to come over.

As I approached him, he sat back on his heels casually, his hands dropping in front of him. "Where are you going now?" he asked.

"Home," I responded emphatically. "It's a long drive back to school." He seemed genuinely concerned.

"It's late already, and you look beat. Aren't you afraid you might fall asleep on the drive back?" I had to admit to some apprehension about that. The roadie was very understanding.

"Look," he said, his voice dropping almost to a whisper, "why don't you come back to the hotel with me tonight? You can crash in my room, and get a fresh start in the morning." Though my natural timidity would normally prevent me from accepting his offer, I was growing too weary to put up much of an argument, and in the end I accepted, gratefully.

The Jam were staying at the top floor of a hotel located on the Sunset Strip. After the roadie let me into his room, I crossed to the window and looked out. It appeared as if all of Los Angeles was stretched out before me. It was beautiful. The single light behind me was extinguished; I went back into the room, lay down on the floor by the bed, and using my knapsack as a pillow, closed my eyes.

There was a moment of silence.

"What are you doing on the floor?" I leaned up on one elbow. He was sitting on the side of the bed, and when he caught my eye, he patted the mattress beside him.

"Come on up here," he coaxed. As tempting as the invitation

was, my manners interceded.

"Thank you, but I wouldn't dream of having you sleep on the floor. You take the bed."

Another silence.

"You're not going to sleep on the bed?" A pause. "Come on, you can sleep on the bed."

I smiled to myself. And they said chivalry was dead...

"No, really, it's all right. Thank you anyway. Good night." I lay my head back down, and closed my eyes. After a long minute there was a click, and the radio turned on. It was loud... too loud, especially for this time of night. There was no way I would be able to sleep with that playing. I again raised up on my elbow.

"Excuse me? I don't mean to be picky, but could you turn that down a little? I can't sleep with it on."

The roadie mumbled something under his breath... and turned the radio off. My head had barely hit the knapsack again before I was asleep.

When I awoke the next morning the room was empty. The roadie had gone. I was sorry I hadn't had a chance to thank him again, and made a mental note to send him flowers for his kindness to me.

Standing by the elevator was another roadie. As I pressed the button to go down, he smiled at me.

"Have a good night?"

"Yes, thank you." He chuckled at that.

"Yeah, I bet."

I wasn't sure why, but I had the feeling he was being rude. As the elevator arrived on my floor, his smile turned into a leer. I was glad when the doors closed between us.

# 6

I would be graduating soon, and knew exactly what I wanted to do - there was only one thing I *could* do! I was going to work at Slash magazine.

It didn't matter what kind of work it was, whether typing or filing or answering phones. Oh heck, if all they needed was a gofer to bring them coffee all day long, I was their girl. As far as my four years' worth of study and credits...I took my knowledge of Greek history and Louis Leakey and the Palace at Versailles, and filed it in my brain under the heading To Be Deleted.

How to get the job had me stumped until I hit on the idea of working there as a volunteer. I had some savings to fall back on, at least for a while, and a small company like Slash might need an extra hand - especially one that was free. It wasn't much to offer, but it was all I had.

I dialed the number listed in the magazine, and after several rings one of their writers answered. He said his name was Chris; he listened as I spelled out my idea, and then repeated it back to me in a puzzled voice. Work at Slash, but not get paid? I held my breath while he silently questioned my sanity, then exhaled as I was passed off to Bob Biggs. So far so good. I repeated my offer to Mr. Biggs, and tried to stay calm as he responded with interest to my query. Then he offered me an appointment to meet him! I couldn't believe it - I had a chance!

The next morning I bathed in my orange juice, drank my shampoo, and headed for Hollywood. My roommate Evon watched me sail down the stairs; a Springsteen fan, she called out teasingly "If you see Bruce, tell him I say hi!"

I checked into a small hotel off Sunset Boulevard. Slash was located further south, on Beverly. It was a modest building, one of those older Los Angeles storefronts, with a one-man drug store downstairs, and offices above. Slash Magazine took over the upstairs floor. There was a long, narrow staircase which led to a small waiting room, which itself was surrounded by several smaller offices. The final feature was a flat roof; accessed only by a wooden window frame, it provided a place to stretch your legs and breathe in the smog.

Mr. Biggs was not what I expected for a punk rock editor. He was soft-spoken and good-humored, with a face that was pure Nebraska farm boy. He graciously invited me into his cramped office, and gave me the chance to convince him why he should hire me. As I spoke he listened politely. I have no idea what he thought of me. Nine-tenths enthusiasm and one-tenth awe, I assured him that I would do anything that needed to be done, no matter how grubby or insignificant or boring or... He suddenly looked like someone who got the joke, but still couldn't quite believe it. I caught my breath, collected my thoughts, and then spoke the words that were in my heart.

"Mr. Biggs, I want to work at Slash more than anything in the world."

I got the job.

Later on that night I decided to go to one more punk gig before making the return trek to Santa Barbara the next day. The small hotel where I was staying had grown quiet; the lobby was empty except for two men entering the hotel. They passed right by me, speaking in low tones. One of the men was short and slender and dark. I was startled to see him, and was almost to the door before

I remembered my promise.

"Hey, Bruce!!"

Bruce Springsteen stopped just short of the elevator, and turned to me.

"Evon says hi!" I shouted.

My pledge to my roommate completed, I spun on my heels and went out the door. If I had paused on the way to the gig for a moment of reflection, perhaps I would have recognized the encounter as a premonition... a premonition that the strangeness was just beginning.

# 7

Over the next few months I worked one to two days a week at Slash, doing whatever needed to be done. In the beginning I didn't even get a chair, which just added to the charm of the place. I sat on the floor, cross legged, and laid out the piles of public relations material in front of me. Biggs was a good boss, but there were days when his patience was tested - like when I came to work five consecutive days with five different hair colors. The only time he sternly put his foot down was when I came in with chains wrapped around the bottoms of my sneakers. They kept putting dents in the wood floor.

And then there was Kickboy. His dark, grizzled face spoke of long nights spent debating the ironies and intricacies of life; it's likely then the waves of hero-worship wafting across the waiting room just irritated the hell out of him. I did try to stay out from underfoot, however, and bother him as little as possible, all the while hoping for the opportunity to speak with him, or do something for him.

Finally my chance arrived. Kickboy came in and began to speak to me, then changed his mind and left the room. Then he came back in. Then he went back out. Well, this was different. I leaned as far across the doorway as I dared; he was there, in the waiting room, and appeared to be wrestling with a decision. It came quicker than I expected, and I had to scramble to make it back to my spot on the floor.

Kickboy nodded to me; my breath held, I rose slowly... a mere serving girl standing before the Crown Prince .... In his heavy French accent he inquired "How would you like to do something illegal?"

"Sure!" I cried happily.

It was the moment I had been waiting for. As it turned out he just wanted me to make a phone call... but that didn't matter; the important thing was, the ice was broken! My joy, however, proved to be short-lived. Within the month Philomena (his girlfriend and one of Slash's founders) moved back to her native London, and Kickboy soon joined her. I mourned his absence. Crossing the waiting room would never be the same.

The other people at Slash were writers Chris D. and Mark Williams, and Robyn.

Robyn was Biggs' Gal Friday, head of marketing, and my immediate boss. With her bouncy, shoulder-length dark hair, 'cat' sunglasses, and slender build fit into impossibly tight jeans, she looked like a SoCal version of Diana Rigg. Beautiful and fun, she mesmerized everyone (especially men) who met her.

On Fridays, as work ended for the day, Robyn would put X's new album 'Los Angeles' on Slash's potent sound system, and crank it up. 'Sex and Dying in High Society' or 'Johnny Hit and Run Pauline' would fill all the rooms. Biggs preferred to listen to Hank Williams Sr., but he never objected to our Friday afternoon punk hootenanny. I can't imagine what the druggist downstairs thought of it. I thought it was glorious.

My role eventually evolved into that of receptionist; my duties included announcing all visitors to Biggs' office (though things at Slash being so informal, visitors rarely stopped for my permission to enter). By then I had both a chair and a desk, but Biggs' attempts to get me to use the new intercom system failed... after all, he *was* just a few feet away. It was much easier to shout "Hey, Biggs! X is here!"

In addition to the magazine, Slash had formed their own record label, with bands that included X, The Germs, and Fear. At one point the Go-Go's were considering signing with Slash. Started by a group of punks hanging around Hollywood, they eventually learned how to play their instruments, and developed their own irresistible sound. I met one of the band members in the office; since I was staying at a motel she kindly offered me a place to stay, but once again my shyness interceded, and I declined.

The deal must have fallen through, because not long after the Go-Go's signed a contract with rival IRS Records. They struck gold with their very first record; entitled Beauty and the Beat, it was a runaway hit. After that, Biggs kept the Go-Go's record album hanging on his wall. He used it as a dartboard.

The best part about Slash was hearing footsteps coming up the stairs. One would never know who it would be! It could be the Blasters, Fear's Lee Ving, or John Doe and Exene from X. In my opinion X was the most impressive group on Slash's roster. John Doe had a strong, melodic voice, and the lyrics he wrote were insightful; Exene was rougher than John, more edgy and wild. They were far and away my favorite band.

The first time X came up the stairs, I gasped.

"Hi!" I cried buoyantly, and a little too loudly.

Exene's mouth, a black gash on a pale background, pursed together; her eyes focused on me, and after a brief, bored assessment, her glance slid away. She moved towards Biggs' office without a word. John Doe went past me as if I was wallpaper. It was a thrilling experience.

My favorite musician to come up the stairs was Lee Ving, of the band Fear. He was older than most punk musicians - maybe even in his thirties. He had the look and attitude of a tough street fighter, and on stage held a well-deserved reputation for being fierce and crude. But he was also the only musician who didn't think it was beneath him to stop and chat with a receptionist. That said more about him than any interview ever did.

When work ended, I went to whatever gig was around. Few bands had the money to advertise in the newspapers, especially when they were playing at a VFW or Mason's hall, or some dive in east L.A. Musicians took to making up their own flyers and posting them on telephone poles around town - that became the best way to find out when a band was playing.

I liked to dance at the gigs. Punk rockers had a unique dance, to say the least. Some writer gave it the term 'slamdancing'. To an outsider it must have seemed crazy, even dangerous, but it wasn't really. It's just that the music could create this volcano of energy inside of you, one that grew and grew until it erupted in a cacophony of elbows and fists and knees.

While it was mostly guys you would see hurling themselves about the floor, there were a handful of girls who dared to slam. I took some pride in being one of those girls; even so, slamdancing rarely caused more damage than a few bruises. Besides, the guys seemed to sense when a girl was dancing, and they would try to protect her.

A lot of times when the dancers collided they would fall into a crowded heap on the floor. One night I found myself at the bottom of one of those piles. I lay there, unable to free myself, while around me swirled a blur of motorcycle boots, embellished with chains and colorful bandanas; the thumping base sounded dim, and far away. Suddenly a strong arm reached down and yanked me up and out, literally pulling me off my feet. The punk checked me out quickly, making sure I was okay - then he gave my head a rough, admiring rub, and shoved me back into the pit. It was the greatest compliment a guy could have given me.

Black Flag was headlining with The Adolescents at a hall in East Hollywood, called Baces. There wasn't too much dancing that night. The floor was soaked and sticky with beer, resulting in more slipping than anything else. At one point my feet slid out from under me, and I went down hard; when I turned to get up, a boot accidentally came down on the back of my shirt. There was a short tug, and then a rip, and the entire back of my shirt tore away. It didn't worry me, though; the front of my shirt was still intact, and after all, that was the side that mattered.

Black Flag were on stage now, but their set had barely gotten started when the electricity to their guitars was shut off. It was then that I heard the shout - the one that warned us that the cops were coming in.

I went out a side door and made my way towards the front of the building. Around the corner was a street filled to capacity with squad cars. I quickly counted - six... a dozen... two dozen, maybe? I couldn't believe it. All of these cops... for us? There was something different about them, as well - the uniforms appeared to be black, not the usual blue, and the white helmets had a plastic shield that came down over their face. Each and every officer was holding his billy club out in front of him.

It triggered a memory of something I had read not long ago - something in Slash... The Elk's Lodge. This is how they looked at the Elk's Lodge! These were riot cops! As I passed two of the officers there was a bark of laughter, and with chagrin I remembered my bare back. But my self-consciousness quickly paled in comparison to what was forming before me.

The cops had created a line, one that reached from one sidewalk across the street to the other. They stood side by side, not moving, though it must have been a powerful gravitational force that kept them from doing so. As the kids came out of the club they saw what was happening, but they didn't run away. One by one they crossed into the street, creating an identical line to the police, parallel to them and about fifty yards away. This would be no Elk's Lodge.

The Baces Hall punks were making a stand.

At first the two sides watched each other with sober measure. I took my place near the front of the crowd of punks. I suppose I should have been afraid, but my curiousity overrode any fear. I wanted to see what was going to happen; I mean, let's face it - *this* was exciting! The situation deteriorated quickly, however, as jeers and taunts were bellowed at the officers, and I began to worry that I had made the wrong choice. I remember thinking, maybe we should all just walk away... it's probably not too late to just... Then a bottle flew, and the chance for a second chance was gone.

The column of cops exploded at us, and punk rockers scattered like ducks at the sound of buckshot. Except for one. Where once a large group of boisterous youths faced down the cops, there now stood one slight girl; my eyes bulged at what appeared to be the entire Los Angeles police department barrelling towards me. I made a kind of squeaking sound, and then some primal sense of self-preservation, or sanity, took hold of me. I ran.

Instead of following the other punks I went perpendicular, down an isolated alley. That was my salvation. The action had gone elsewhere, as almost everyone else had raced north up the street. As I pulled myself over a barbed wire fence the police grabbed those unlucky few who were too slow or too drunk to get away. My boots slipped on the metal fence and I tumbled onto a dark lane. It was quiet there; no one had followed me. I wandered past the gated yards and the occasional excited, baying dog, until I found myself on a main street. I was then able to doubleback to my car, and head for home.

The next morning there was no mention of a riot in the main press, at least none that I could find. I hoped no one had been hurt.

After breakfast I considered the damage. I've never been the kind of girl who likes to shop; I'd sooner defrost the refrigerator than try on clothes. But sometimes a girl has to do what a girl has to do, no matter how unpleasant, so the next morning I dragged myself to the nearest department store and gave in to necessity. I bought a shirt.

Back in Santa Barbara I read that the Germs would be reuniting on December 3rd, for one last show at the Starwood.

Darby Crash was already a punk legend in Los Angeles; his

songs were powerful, and his live performances were said to be even more wild, if not chaotic. Darby was known to roll around on stage on broken glass, or stalk around the platform like an uncaged animal. I myself had never actually seen The Germs, so I was thrilled at finally having this chance. Then I saw my calender. December 4th. I had a final on December 4th, one that I really needed to study for. Damn. There was just no way I could go out the night before that test...

Darby was pacing back and forth across the Starwood's stage. I couldn't tell what he was singing about - not that it mattered; neither could anyone else. His lyrics had always been like an audio Rorschach test; everyone heard what they wanted to hear.

After the first couple of songs, my attention wandered towards the crowd behind me. As Darby snarled and writhed I walked towards the back, near the tables; The Germs faded into the background, but their music became the soundtrack for the adventure that lay before me.

Between songs, I literally bumped into Leslie. Sweet-faced, bespectacled, and outgoing, she returned my smile and right away began to talk to me. She spoke with the ease of someone who loved people and had an open, trusting heart. Leslie also loved punk rock music, and told me she was looking for a place to live in Los Angeles.

It was one of those moments in life that, on reflection, you realize was just meant to be. Within a span of not more than five minutes, I had found my roommate. We exchanged phone numbers, and I told her I'd call her as soon as I got to Hollywood. Just one more final, and my college career was completed. Not that I cared- Slash was waiting for me, and Los Angeles, and the excitement of living as a punk rocker. I went back to Santa Barbara later that evening.

Four days later, Darby Crash killed himself.

# 8

St. Andrews Place, Hollywood. As the landlady took my check for the first and last month's rent, I looked out from the front porch with satisfaction.

It was an abbreviated, quiet street, wedged between Sunset and Hollywood Boulevards. There were only a handful of houses; the majority of them were older, and just teetering on the brink of compelled renovation. Not exactly poor, but hardly middle class, the homes were somewhere in-between; it was as if the street were its own Brigadoon, caught between two worlds. Each one had a mature tree in front, offering a respite from the sun. Behind us was an elementary school, from which came the sounds of laughter and ringing bells.

Our house was a duplex, split into identical halves, with both units sharing a large, cement front porch. It was built during World War II, back when people relaxed on their porches on the weekend, waving to the neighbors and commenting on the weather that rarely changed. Though the rooms were cramped, and the few appliances ancient, the house had a warm, welcoming feeling, like visiting a favorite old aunt. I loved it.

There was a small living room just as you entered the house, with a well-worn brown carpet that spoke of multiple and determined cleanings. The kitchen allowed us one tiny table and two modest chairs, with just enough space to pour milk on cereal without bumping an elbow. The house boasted of two bathrooms, though the one downstairs appeared to me to be more of a closet enclosing an endlessly running toilet.

Upstairs was a roomier bathroom, with an actual shower, and the two bedrooms. Leslie took the larger one, facing the street, which was fine with me. I liked my small bedroom; it smelled sweetly of wood floors and freshly soaped walls. I would lay on my bed and close my eyes, and listen as the joyful noises from the schoolyard wafted in on the soft breeze.

One day I was upstairs in my bedroom when Leslie came home early. Leslie had the rare (to me) ability for instantly making friends, a trait I both envied and admired; when she called up that she had someone she wanted me to meet, I hopped off my bed and went to the top of the stairs to greet the visitor. And froze. Short, pale skin, black hair... it was her. It was *her*. The girl, the one with the lighter. The gremlin.

Leslie escorted her out the window of the bedroom to the porch overhang. For a moment I considered going in the opposite direction, but instead crawled under the old wooden sill to join them. The breeze drifted about the overhang, with a delicate December smell that reminded me of early spring. Uncertain and more than a little nervous, I glanced over at our guest. Her face was turned up to the sky, trying to catch the bits of sunlight that escaped between the leaves of the trees, and all of a sudden she seemed... younger. She caught me watching her, and smiled.

Her name was Bobbi Brat. She was Leslie's friend. And in the months ahead, she would become mine.

# 9

There was an unspoken camaraderie among punk rockers, even when they didn't know each other. I was reminded of that one night on the way to a concert.

Leslie and I were in my car. I guess I wasn't paying attention, and as we approached a red light, we banged into the VW Bug in front of us. Well, not banged, exactly - more like bumped. Bumped gently. That distinction probably wasn't going to help me much, though; when the heavy-set young woman with the shaved head and mohawk exited the Bug with the slam of a door, it appeared that she wasn't going to be interested in my excuses. At that point I debated whether I should reach for my insurance card, or just roll up the window and pray.

She walked to the driver's side window, put her forearms on the car door, and squatted down. It was then that I recognized her; though we had never spoken with each other, we had been at several of the same gigs. Her name was Shirley.

She glanced at Leslie's dyed hair, and our punk clothes; as I opened my mouth to attempt an apology, Shirley shrugged and said nonchalantly, "Oh, okay." And returned to her car. That was it. There were no accusations, no fights. She didn't know us - but we were punks. That was all she needed to know. Sitting scrunched down in my car, watching her drive away... for the first time, I felt I belonged.

The Bug plodded its awkward way up to the red traffic light, music blasting through the closed windows. Another car was already waiting there, and we pulled up behind it. Except for the three vehicles, the street was empty.

Suddenly the doors of the Volkswagon burst open, and Shirley and her two companions jumped out and began slamdancing right there in the street. Heads low. Knees high. Elbows pumping. This was crazy! Slamming in a dance club was one thing... but in the middle of the street? It was bizarre, and stupid, and... wonderful. The light returned to green, the kids hurled themselves back inside without skipping a beat, and off they went.

The car in front of us didn't budge. I waited a moment, then gingerly, almost apologetically, edged my way around it and past. I drove for a few seconds, then peered in my rear view mirror; the car was still there, its driver frozen. The light turned red again.

# 10

When people describe punk rock, words like anger, belligerence, and rage are often used... but no one could have applied those to me. In January of 1981, I was one happy punk rocker! I was working at Slash, I had a wonderful roommate, and my nights were filled with punk concerts. After a while my life took on a kind of routine - work, supper, then somewhere, a gig. When Leslie and I headed out that night, I assumed I knew what lay ahead of me. I was wrong.

I hadn't heard of any gigs going on, so we took the car and drove towards the Whiskey, hoping something interesting would turn up along the way. As we travelled west down Sunset Boulevard we passed two punk rockers; one of them had a mohawk that was stiff and purple and of a remarkable height. The boys were standing beside a police car, and appeared to be answering questions. Though we were curious about what was happening, we thought it wiser to just keep going.

There was a band playing at the Whiskey, but it wasn't punk rock, just some lame New Wave crossover. 'New Wave' was supposedly a combination of punk and pop, but its true purpose was to make program managers feel like they were open to new music, without actually having to acknowledge what was really happening.

And what was happening was punk rock.

Like the fifteen year olds who flocked to the gigs, punk rock was younger, harder, and faster than any of its progenitors. It was the skateboard wheel grinding on the edge of a swimming pool, and the teenage boy's hand shoved away for groping previously unchartered territories. New Wave, on the other hand, was... reassuring. Promoters could book the bands with little fear of a riot. Its musicians could be invited to corporate parties, without making fools of themselves in front of music executives and their wives. Elvis Costello, The Talking Heads, and Blondie were New Wave bands. X, The Adolescents, and Black Flag were not. I'm not sure at what point rock rebellion had morphed into conformity, but it was a virus invading the record industry.

On that December evening, however, I wasn't thinking about the unfairness of the music business or the cowardice of radio program managers. The night had been a bust. We were on our way home already when we passed those same two punks. Leslie, with her warm heart and penchant for picking up strays, suggested that we stop and make sure they were all right. The car eased over beside them.

"Hey!" Leslie's brightly colored head leaned out the window. "Hey! Yeah, I mean you! Come over here!"

The boy with the shorter Mohawk approached us cautiously. He looked to be about seventeen.

"Need a lift?"

Without a word the two boys hopped into the back seat, and I pulled away from the curb. Leslie chatted easily with Perry and Joe, and she soon learned that they needed a place to crash for the night. They might have been runaways, or maybe just directionless - living out on the street until they came up with a better plan. It was all right with me if they spent the night, though I suspected my approval didn't matter all that much. Leslie had already told them they could stay.

By the time we got home it was almost midnight, and I was bushed. Leslie, on the other hand, was just getting started; she was determined to find a gig, and her new friends offered to go with her. Once they left I went upstairs to my room, and crashed within minutes. Usually I'm a light sleeper, waking to the slightest unusual sound. I guess that night I was more tired than I knew.

The next morning I woke and got dressed, as I had every other morning. I pulled on my jeans and ran my hand through my hair, just like every morning. Then I went downstairs and watched my routine implode and collapse back onto itself, like so much nuclear fallout. Before me, crashed in a sleeping bag on our living room floor, was Perry. And Joe. And fifteen complete strangers.

Our little living room was covered end to end with sleeping bags and sheets and blankets; barely an inch of carpet was visible underneath all the bodies. For a second I thought this might be some weird cosmic punk mirage, but after a couple of blinks they were still there. At that point my lessons kicked in.

When I was young, we would often have visitors from all over the world; instructions in etiquette and courtesy thus became essential. 'Always endeavor to put a guest at ease'... that was an early lesson. 'Mucho gusto' was a friendly and proper greeting, instilled in me well before 'abre la ventana'. And while a man's hand was shaken firmly, a woman's would guide the amount of pressure imposed. These were cherished skills, ones that I took seriously and practiced with pride. The beauty and clarity of rules were comforting to me; even as a little kid, I would color my pictures within the established lines. It had become a part of my nature.

'Always put a guest at ease'. That may explain why, when I found my floor covered with strangers, I didn't raise my voice, or shake one of them awake, or even gently nudge one of the new houseguests with my toe. I instead navigated the body-laden carpet with the skill of a tightrope artist, and reached the empty kitchen without disturbing a soul.

At work I typed and sorted, I answered phones and greeted visitors, I went to lunch and came back from lunch and all the while I wondered who the hell all those people were! Not surprisingly, they made for a day-long distraction, which led to more than one work mistake on my part. Yet mixed in with the uncertainty was this wonderful curiousity, and a thrilling sense of anticipation.

Who <u>were</u> those people?

When the afternoon finally crawled to the five o'clock hour, I raced back to the house. A young woman greeted me there; about my age, or perhaps a little older, she wore a flannel shirt with a long baggy skirt. Her most striking feature, however, was her hair; she had the most amazing set of dreadlocks I had ever seen. They were thick, and long, and beautiful. She said her name was Malissa. As we sat outside on the porch talking, one of her companions returned, and then another, and that was how I was introduced to the TC.

TC. It stood for 'The Connected'. They were a group of kids who had banded together for survival, the name implying both protection and friendship. I suppose they could have been considered a gang, but they were much more like a big, extended family. There were Mark and Lane, Critter and Rachel. I learned that Maggie and Emil were a couple, as were Brian and Stephanie, and Ricky and Gloria. With the exception of Malissa, who was one year older than I, the TC were young, some as young as fifteen. Malissa explained to me that there were other TC spread out around Los Angeles, as well; they would come in and out of our lives in the months ahead, sometimes with a profound effect.

The kids had been squatting in a house with Darby Crash, but they had since lost that place, and were now out in the street. Malissa, speaking for the group, asked if they could stay, at least for awhile.

I, speaking from years of loneliness, said yes.

# 11

The next few weeks made up for six vacant years. The TC had become an instant, extended family to me, and I quickly learned that no matter where I went, whether it was to a gig in Huntington Beach or a party in Venice... if a member of The Connected was there, I was welcome.

Interestingly enough, the TC looked quite different from the stereotypical L.A. punk. Most of the punk rockers in Los Angeles had a kind of uniform. The boys wore straightleg jeans with biker boots, which they wrapped with chains and several worn but brightly colored bandanas. Sometimes they tied a Pendleton shirt around their narrow hips, while others took to wearing kilts over their jeans - a really cool look. The punk rock girls donned much the same clothes, though they would usually add a pair of suspenders, and substitute a short, Catholic schoolgirl skirt for the pants. Spiked hair was still popular, though more and more an ultra-short cut could be seen. In those cases a few long strands of hair would usually remain - a last holdover of traditional femininity - though they would not escape the outrageous effects of home-made food dye.

The TC were different. Three of the kids wore their hair in long dreadlocks. The boys wore loose pants, button down or tee shirts, and Converse sneakers. The girls were more inventive - it's as if their wardrobe had become a reflection of their imagination and independence (and for a person like myself, who wore the same outfit for several days in a row, this was an epiphany). During the day they scoured the thrift shops, buying mismatched outfits, and ball gowns, and fifties-style dresses, and then went to work on them. The result was a look that was still punk, and yet their own. I began to copy the TC girls, and thus added my own touch - a little white cotton dress, to accompany my biker boots.

So much was happening at St. Andrews now, I hardly knew in which direction to turn. Unlike the portrayals of punk 'crash pads' as dens of vacant, lazy miscreants, the house was filled with energy and wit. The girls might be in the kitchen together cooking breakfast for the group, or off alone in a corner somewhere, drawing in a notebook. Some of them, notably Tova and Malissa, appeared to be natural-born artists; Tova's clothing designs were scattered about the living room, and occasionally a beautiful horse head drawn by Malissa would peek out from under a book. The boys would often get in spirited, good-natured wrestling matches, attacking each other like newly awakened puppies. This sort of physical closeness was new to me, and I desperately wanted to join in, as Maggie and Stephanie and Gloria did so easily. But my shyness was a straightjacket that kept me in my corner; I watched their intimacy with a kind of hunger.

Emil and Mark were skateboarders, and since I also loved to skate, and was a natural-born tomboy, I journeyed along with them. Emil became sort of a little brother to me. One of the youngest of the TC, he had blue eyes, blond dreadlocks, a flat nose, and just about the widest grin I'd ever seen. In time I learned to be cautious of that grin, and the glint in his eyes that usually accompanied it, for it meant we were about to do something we probably shouldn't. Whether it was scaling a barbed wire fence to skate a forbidden parking lot, or driving the wrong way down an alley, or sneaking into a club through a broken window, Emil was my guide.

As the older one I sometimes felt I should chastise him, or at least share with him the wisdom of my experience... but then he would sling an affectionate arm about my shoulders and pull me to him in a childlike hug, and I knew I would follow him anywhere.

I loved Mark too, but in a whole other way. Mark was the lead singer for a band called The Oziehares. As soon as I met him I was instantly head over heels. The handsome nineteen year old had an easy charm, which was only enhanced by his apparent ignorance of it. Usually funny and playful, at other times he would be enveloped by introspection, with an intensity that was almost frightening. More than anything else in the world, I wanted Mark to love me, but it wasn't long before I realized that that was not going to happen.

It appeared that the main qualification to date him was an intangible blend of beauty and fragility; I, unfortunately, had neither. As his lack of interest became clear I tried to put up a wall around my feelings, but without much luck. Despite my fervent wish that he never know of my crush, I managed to sabotage myself with sad, lovesick gazes and the occasional hopeful smile. But if Mark was aware of how I felt, he thankfully never let on.

Over the weekend we made a trip down to Huntington Beach, where I was introduced to Mark's older brother. I recognized him right away; I'd seen his photo in the skating magazines. Tony was one of the 'Dogtown' crew - the skaters who had started the trend of sneaking into and shredding any backyard swimming pools that residents were foolhardy enough to leave dry.

Tony was taller and heavier than Mark, with black, unruly hair and a tanned, rugged face. The day I met him, he was trying a new move on a cement block in a parking lot. Each time he attempted it, he failed, and the board would skid out across the pebble-strewn pavement. I don't know where I got the nerve, but I raised my voice and teasingly offered to show him how it was done. That got his attention! Most guys would have been embarassed by that, or even defensive, so it was a surprise to see the amused grin that spread across his face.

A couple of weeks later, I think prompted by the TC, Tony gave me one of his boards to keep as my own. Running my hand down the wide, rough surface in awe, I couldn't wait to try it out. As it happened, I was a little too excited, and morning came without my seeing even an hour of sleep. Nevertheless, I eagerly accepted Tony's invitation to hunt out a new location to skate. As we drove up into the hills, I waited for him to pull into an isolated street, or perhaps park near an unused swimming pool.

Twenty minutes later we were standing on top of a rugged hill, looking down into a cement drainage tube. The names of several punk bands were spraypainted on its side, indicating that this was a popular spot with skateboarders. But while this sort of a thing was a walk in the park for him, I'd never skated anything like it before; wimping out with Tony watching, however, was not an option, so I peered over the edge again. Its sides sloped up sharply enough, but then they rounded off gently at the top. Oh, okay. This wouldn't be too hard, after all. I was even a little disappointed that he had picked something so... well, hackneyed.

Underestimating Tony was something most people did only once, and it was a lesson I was about to learn. He was already shredding on his board - but not on the cement. On the hillside. On a hillside composed entirely of dirt, rocks, and the odd boulder. That day he showed me that, if you can imagine it, you can skate just about anything.

One afternoon Mark, Emil and I were ripping on the schoolyard at Kenter Elementary when Emil suddenly disappeared. Later that evening, the household was blessed with a weekend's worth of hamburger meat, buns, and supplies. Emil had found a way into the school's kitchen, and did some selective pilfering. After some initial uneasiness I told myself that this was okay because, after all, the food was meant to be eaten by kids... and we were kids. Admittedly it was a long leap to make, but I managed it. The next day, however, Oziehares flyers began to appear in multiples, and I realized that food was not the only thing that had suddenly disappeared from Kenter. We now were the not-so-proud owners of a copy machine, also formerly known as Property of the Los Angeles School District. It was harder for me to justify *that*, but it didn't stop me from trying; eventually I even allowed myself to eat a hamburger.

As the days went by I slowly got to know more of the TC family. Because of my own timidity, it was the more outgoing members that I came to know first. Stephanie was the youngest of the girls, and an exhuberant companion; dark-haired and pretty, she had a matter-of-fact awareness of her own radiating sexuality. Her boyfriend Brian had short-cropped blond hair and a ready grin. Malissa was soft-spoken and gentle, with a natural warmth; she was the sort of person that you wanted to bring your fears to for comfort, and your accomplishments to for praise. But of all the kids I met, it was Maggie with whom I developed the strongest bond.

Maggie had the most unique look I had ever seen. She had shoulder-length black dreadlocks that occasionally hid her eyes, but rarely obscured a dazzling smile. Her outfits usually included plaid pants and black men's shoes; several times, when walking down Melrose Avenue, men (and women) would pull over to admire her. The most surprising accessory, however, was her round, red earring - which she wore in her nose. We called it 'the big red zit'.

I sometimes wondered why Maggie never tried modeling, but like a lot of the kids down here, it seemed that she didn't know what path to take. She reminded me a little of a spinning top - all energy, but with no real direction. But either way, she was hypnotic. Maggie dressed as she liked, spoke as she liked, and did what she wanted, whether socially acceptable or not. Her energy and irreverance turned heads wherever she went.

When I first met Maggie at the house I realized I knew her, or rather I knew her face. A drawing of her had appeared earlier that week on the cover of The LA Weekly. The picture exuded hostility and disdain. Her grim appearance glared out at the readers, challenging them - no, *daring* them to judge her. Underneath her the caption read 'This Violent Generation', and upon seeing her expression there were few who would doubt its veracity. But the girl who stood before me now was unrecognizable when compared to that snarling image, and though I'm not exactly sure why, I felt completely at ease with her.

That confidence may explain why I agreed to let Maggie cut my hair. It had been getting steadily shorter anyway, and I figured she must know what she was doing... As I sat calmly in the chair she studied the shape of my head like a modern-day Michelangelo, the electric razor buzzing eagerly in her hand.

There is a curiously unsettling sensation in the interior of one's stomach that most women have felt when getting their hair cut. In this instance, it wasn't the sight of my hair trickling into my lap that unnerved me, or even the distasteful vibration of the razor against my scalp. Nope, what got my heart racing was hearing Maggie murmur "Oops."

Oops?

I jumped up and grabbed a hand mirror - staring back at me was what a veterinarian would surely have diagnosed as a classic case of mange. My head had been turned into a patchwork of short spikes and bald spots; those hairs that did remain stood up stiffly, like little soldiers at attention. But as I turned my head from side to side my heartbeat began to slow, and to my barber's relief, I finally grinned. Yeah. Perfect. It was perfect.

Now that my hair was short, I decided to bleach it white, as well. No one else around me had my look, except for the occasional senior citizen. The best part of it was finding my own style, so different from everyone else's. Well... that, and the fact that it also cut down considerably on my time under a blow dryer. It was so short that by the time I exited a shower, my hair was already dry. It wouldn't have to be curled, or straightened, or thrown it into an exasperated ponytail. I was free.

But my outfit was not yet complete. When I was growing up, my favorite book was The Outsiders by S. E. Hinton, and there was a scene in the book where Ponyboy and Johnny played chicken by holding lit cigarettes to each other's wrist. They kept the cigarettes there, despite the pain, waiting for the other to yell 'uncle'. It sounded like a wild and adventurous thing to do.

Deciding this for myself, of course, was one thing; finding someone to play chicken *with* me was something else entirely. Gloria passed, Joni only laughed and walked away, and Maggie thought it was the dumbest idea she'd heard in a long time. It was Malissa who gave me my chance.

But not at chicken. She offered instead to give me a Germs burn. I hesitated; I knew what that was. Darby had started a tradition whereby his friends and fans used a cigarette to burn a circle on their inner left wrist. It signified loyalty to him, and allegiance, and, perhaps most importantly, it would be permanent. Darby knew that twenty years later, when one of us was shopping at the market with our kids, we would hand a twenty to the clerk, look down, see the scar, and remember. Remember him, remember the Germs. Maybe just remember a time when we were wild enough and stupid enough to burn a hole in ourselves. Only someone who had a Germs burn, could give a Germs burn. That was the rule. Malissa had her Germs burn.

That wasn't exactly what I had in mind, but I did like the band, and it was an honor, especially coming from Malissa. Besides, once she had offered, it would have been rude to have refused. I took a breath and nodded.

Malissa reached over for a cigarette that had been left sitting half-abandoned in its tray. She placed its tip on the inside of my left wrist, and bringing her lips down close to my skin, blew softly. I watched the end glow and waited nervously for the anticipated pain, but there was actually very little. It stung a bit, that's all. After a minute or so she announced that it was done, and went back into the kitchen.

I examined my prize. It was small and round and raw. Later it would turn black before peeling off entirely, leaving a pale scar behind.

As far as games of chicken went, it was closer to solitaire than poker, but that didn't really matter. I had my Germs burn. It would stand as an indelible memory, whenever I reached over and paid for that carton of milk.

# 12

The Oziehares were playing a gig at the Vex - a dark, rundown hall in an East L.A. neighborhood. The residents of that area were primarily Mexican; the houses that lined the street were small, but tidy. Across from the hall was a bar; whenever its front door opened, lighthearted trumpet music would escape, and then grow muffled once again.

I suppose it wasn't very smart for a group of punked-out white kids to show up in this part of town, and at this time of night. But besides the invincibility of youth that most teenagers share, there was also the small fact that concert halls in Los Angeles weren't exactly lining up to showcase punk bands. Balancing off the money to be made was the awareness that property damage, or even a riot (however unlikely), could ensue. If the club owners were willing to take the risk,the bands were not going to back out. So they went where the opportunity took them, kept a wary eye on their equipment, avoided fights as much as possible, and got the hell out.

The Oziehares were still usually listed at the bottom of the ticket, but their following was growing. Emil was an amazing drummer, and Mark's natural presence and energy were amplified onstage. Yet while Lane proved to be a steady bass player, they had trouble finding, and keeping, a lead guitarist. Tonight it was a girl guitar player who stepped in - I didn't know her name, but she was fast.

As the Oziehares began to set up I mulled about backstage. The guest room was small and dirty, with a couch so stained that the original color was hard to discern. Maggie was there, along with two TC that I had just recently met. Tova was in her early twenties; she was dark and curvaceous, with an intelligent sophistication about her. Her friend Drew appeared to be the opposite of herself. He was years younger than Tova, and his demeanor was quite different; Drew was ebullient, almost goofy - like a court jester on helium.

Tova was dryly complaining to Maggie about the grafitti on the walls. She was annoyed to find her name scrawled there; accompanied by crude drawings, they were primarily comments about what Tova allegedly wanted to do to a certain part of Drew's anatomy. Maggie turned to Tova and playfully began to interview her.

"Tova, what do you think of the slogans that say 'Tova likes to suck Drew's cock at the Vex'?"

Tova looked up at the vulgarities, and mustered a smile. "Do you mean that one there, or that one up there?"

Drew couldn't resist that opportunity; he jumped up and pointed cheerfully to his crotch. "No, she means this one right here!"

The light-hearted teasing continued for a few more minutes, until we heard the signature opening chords of Lane's base. The Oziehares' gig had begun.

Their songs were fast, ferocious. Emil attacked the drums in a controlled frenzy, while Mark hurled himself about the stage, the microphone a conduit for his anger. 'Feelin Trapped', 'Get Outta My Brain', 'Why Don't You Leave', 'Skank Her Poon' - the Oziehares' songs gave words to Mark's frustrations, and more pointedly, to the women who created those frustrations. I was envious of the girls who inspired Mark's lyrics.

The set went well; the hall wasn't too crowded, but there were enough people there to make the slamdancing fun. At one point a kid, probably drunk, attempted to leap off the stage into the crowd; there weren't enough people to cushion the blow, however, and an uncomfortable *smack* could be heard as he hit the floor.

As Mark, Emil, and Lane finished and began packing up the equipment, the rest of us wandered outside. We stayed close together for the most part, not straying too far from the club; this was an area we rarely visited during the daytime, let alone at night. Just down the street we stopped to peer into a shop window. It appeared to be some sort of a bakery; a sign in Spanish advertised fresh tortillas.

Mark and Lane were carrying their speakers down to the truck; as they passed me I saw an odd sight out of the corner of my eye. There was a man standing in the middle of the street by the club - right in the intersection. He was just standing there, as if in a daze. A car swung widely past him, honking in annoyance, but still the man did not move. Curious, I left the others and walked in his direction.

The door to the entrance was shut; the only people near me were a couple of young punks who I didn't know, a slender Mexican man, and a very, very large bouncer. I kept my eyes on the man in the street. What in the world could he be doing? It didn't take much longer for me to find out.

In a surreal, bizarre rendition of the opening scene from Gunsmoke, the man moved his right arm away from his side in an exaggerated curve, and started slowly approaching the club. As he moved into the orb of light created by a streetlamp, I saw that he was wearing a holster around his waist, and it wasn't empty. For a moment I considered running, but Emil was inside, and I wasn't going to leave him there.

The door was just far enough away to keep me from making a try for it, so I stayed where I was. Never having seen a shootout before, I may have actually been more curious than scared, but at least I had sense enough to squeeze myself between the wall and the bouncer. I had a vague hope that if bullets started flying, they would have to go through a whole lot of meat and fat before they got to me.

I peeked my head around the bouncer in time to see the slender Mexican man, the one who had been sharing the wall with us, run up to the would-be gunslinger. For a full minute he argued with him, but in a tone meant to soothe. After a while the man in the street appeared to give in, albeit reluctantly; he looked almost dejected as he turned, disappearing into the blackness of the night.

The gunfight had ended before it had begun. I wiggled out from behind my unwitting protector, and waited for Emil to emerge from the club.

# 13

And so it went, waking up each day to see what new adventure would unfold. In order to survive in our environment we found it necessary to adopt the tactics of evasion and deceipt - from the cops, from the gangs... and from our landlady.

Mrs. Mangold was a middle-aged woman, but with the energy that came from loving her work. She viewed me with suspicion in the beginning, but eventually my qualifications overruled her uneasiness and (some might say) better judgment. As long as I paid the rent on time, kept the house clean, kept the noise down - and of course, only two people were allowed to live in the house...

As I looked out over my living room floor, the carpet completely covered with multi-colored blankets and sleeping bags, I knew I was going to have a problem. Once in my third year at college, I had to hide a forbidden cat from the prying eyes of a landlord. I managed to pull it off for about two weeks.

One of the boys began to stir; getting to his feet, he accidentally stepped on his neighbor. His victim cursed, and a boot flew across the room, hitting an unintended, and unamused, target. I sighed. This was going to be harder than hiding a cat. A lot harder.

It didn't help that we stuck out like a cockroach at a pest control convention. A week after the TC moved in, a local Mexican gang called White Fence spraypainted their name right on our front porch. It was a greeting card of a sort - not friendly, but not yet hostile. It served to let us know that they ran the street, and they were watching.

Then there was the house across the way. I would be sitting on the front porch, and suddenly there would be movement in one of the windows facing us. The curtain would rustle, just a little, and the dark outline of a face would appear. If I stared at the face long enough, it would duck back behind the protective material. I was starting to feel a little bit paranoid - did this person know the land-lady? If she did, would she tell Mrs. Mangold about all the extra people coming and going? It was one thing to invite, and even enjoy, attention. It was something else entirely to be the focus of prying, unseen eyes.

Added to the mix was the Los Angeles police department. There again, it was fun to be on the outs with the cops - they clear-ly did not like us, and on an impersonal level, the feeling was returned. But we didn't want to provoke the police - we wanted to be left alone.

Pacifying the gang members, dodging the landlady, avoiding the police - it was going to be an interesting game of cat and mouse.

# 14

I needed a nickname. My name was just so... I don't know. Blah. That was it. It was blah.

Besides, a lot of the kids had them - Animal, Mad Dog, Bobbi Brat, Mugger, Critter. Before Pat Smear was Pat, he was George; before Darby Crash was Darby he was Bobby Pyn, and even that wasn't his real name. One had to be careful, though; not all nicknames were good. I mean, even though he was content with his moniker, I wouldn't want to be known as Mr. Potatohead (as one TC was) no matter how affectionately it was used. Nor did I want to be known as Squinty, or Stinky, or any of the other colorful but less-than-complimentary names that could be assigned.

The closest I came to being given a nickname occurred one evening when I was hanging out on a street corner on Sunset Boulevard. A cop in a patrol car pulled up and called me over.

"Hey, Blondie! Yeah, you! I don't want to see you around here no more tonight."

This was very annoying, less for the unfairness of the demand than for what he called me. Blondie? He called me *Blondie*? I was not blonde! Not according to that bottle of super ultra platinum hair bleach, I wasn't! My hair was *white*. On the other hand, it would have been a little odd for a police officer to shout 'Hey, Whitey!' That's just something you don't hear very often.

So back to my search for the perfect punk nickname. Critter

had a great name, but of course that was already taken. It couldn't be too off-the-wall; Tony easily got away with Mad Dog, but no one would believe that of me. Well... what about Kitten? Nah, too Father Knows Best. Sweetpea, perhaps? Nope, same problem - besides, who ever heard of a punk rocker named Sweetpea? Let's see... Emil once said I was 'squirrely'. Squirrely... *Squirrel!*

Uh... no.

Well, what about a play on words, like Pat Smear, and Lorna Doom? I wracked my brain for something witty and clever, something that hadn't been done before. Like... like... like... aarghhh!

Okay, maybe if I fooled around with my own name. Amie. There had to be something I could do with that. Amie... Amie... A -

I had it. I had it!! It was clever, it was catchy - it was punk!

Amie. Ba. A-me. Ba.

Amoeba. A single-celled creature!

That was it! I had found my new nickname. I would be called Amoeba.

It was thus with great satisfaction and joy that I presented my new name to the TC.

There was just one problem.

No one called me that. No one. Not once. Never.

I was to remain plain ol', boring, blah... Amie.

I don't know... maybe I should have gone with Squinty.

# 15

Dressing the way we did, dancing the way we did, being different in an era of conformity... it was a blast. Someone had said that most kids did things to be 'in', but punks did them to be 'out'. I couldn't argue with that. Even that small hint of danger added to the allure of it all. But I never thought anyone would die because of it.

I was upstairs in my back bedroom, putting away the clothes I had just cleaned at the local laundromat. Well, perhaps 'putting away' is not quite accurate. Since I only owned three shirts and two pairs of jeans, they were usually tossed at the nearest chair; more times than not they brushed the chair ever so slightly, before landing in a pile on the floor.

Only a few of the gang were home. Ricky was there, and where you found Ricky, you usually found Gloria. Ricky's girl was slender and pretty; though she wore the usual punk outfit, her mature body and bubbly personality made it almost feminine. Gloria brimmed over with a lively gaiety and charm - while at the same time leaving little doubt that, if needed, she could land a mean right hook.

Joni and Judy were sitting on the floor. They were the first lesbians I had ever met; hell, they were the only lesbians I had ever met. Joni had short hair that stuck out in unruly blue cowlicks; she was a small girl, and quiet, but very tough. Whatever obstacles she encountered in her life, you knew that she met them head-on. Joni wasn't afraid of anything. Judy, on the other hand, was quite different. She was gentle and emotional, with dark eyes that hovered above a fragile smile. It may be true that the strength of a couple lies in the strength of each individual; but if two halves *could* make a whole, that was Judy and Joni.

It was almost midnight when a commotion erupted downstairs; there were muffled shouts, punctuated by cries of alarm. I raced downstairs. Perry was there, standing in the middle of the living room - he was wide-eyed, almost frantic. Joni had a look on her face I hadn't seen before. She was trying to calm Perry down, and as he paced back and forth the story came out.

Perry had been hanging out on a street corner with some friends of his. A car went by, and moments later, they heard gunshots. This was years before the term 'drive-by shooting' became such a recognizable part of the American language; the concept of someone actually being shot was shocking.

"Perry, are you sure? Couldn't it have just been... I don't know, a backfire, or something?"

Perry shook his head impatiently. No, he insisted, they could hear shots fired again right after that, further down the road; then another kid came running up to them, yelling that a punk rocker had been deliberately shot at.

A chill went through me, leaving me suddenly panic-stricken. Where was Maggie? And Emil? Malissa... did she go to Santa Monica tonight, or was it Hollywood? Was Mark still down in Huntington Beach?

Judy began to weep softly, collapsing onto the floor. As Joni went to her side, Perry's anger and frustration overtook him; he slammed his fist into the wall, then pushed himself off and ran out the front door. Ricky shouted to him, and after murmuring something reassuring to Gloria, he ran after Perry.

Looking around the near-empty house, I didn't know what to do. Should I go out and search for my friends, or stay by the phone in case a call came in for an urgent ride out of danger? I finally chose to wait by the phone. It was to be a very long night; in a house devoid of television, books, even furniture, there was little to cause a distraction - we always had been our own distraction. The tension and fear made the hours go by even more slowly. Joni stayed by Judy's side, and Gloria went outside to the porch steps; every few minutes she would scan the street, in the hope of her boyfriend's safe return. After a couple of hours with no news, I went upstairs to my room, to sit in the dark, and wait.

I didn't remember falling asleep. Laying down on my bed, I thought I could still hear Judy's sobs and Joni's hushed assurances, but now the house was still. I sat up, and then nearly jumped; Ricky was on the edge of my bed, his head down, staring at his hands. He could have been there a minute, or an hour.

I studied his profile in silence. Ricky was a tough-looking skinhead, with a wide face and muscular arms. He often dressed like a 'cholo', the local term for a Mexican gangster. He might have been partly Mexican, though I had never asked. I also never asked him about the two teardrops tattooed below his left eye.

The rumor was that as a gang member Ricky had killed people, and then engraved a teardrop on his cheek for each death; others disputed that, arguing that it only stood for each year he had been in jail. I never tried to find out which was the truth. Ricky was funny and kind; he teased me sometimes, and I liked being around him. I didn't want to know.

As I curled my legs underneath me, Ricky suddenly began to speak. His voice was a soft monotone, barely above a whisper; it was as if he were telling a bedtime story to a sleepy child. But his was no nursery tale.

He had lost Perry, and found himself alone on a seemingly deserted street. It was a poor, rundown area - both the convenience store on the corner and the gas station were marked with gang grafitti. Earlier he thought he had heard gunfire, but no longer. Ricky crossed the corner cautiously, alert to the sudden gunning of a car engine, or a figure approaching too quickly.

In the dark he nearly stumbled over the boy. Ricky knelt down beside the motionless form splayed awkwardly on the lawn. The kid was wearing an army jacket with Black Flag scrawled across the back in black marker; Ricky leaned in closer, and it was then that he saw the stained face, and the spiked hair sticky with blood. The kid had been shot in the head.

A warm circle of that blood began to stain the grass beside him. Ricky stood up. He had no choice; he couldn't afford to be found by the body, and there was nothing to be done anyway.

My own head began to feel light; in the hushed silence of the late night, in Ricky's whispered tone and pale expression, the conversation had taken on an unworldly tone. Then without another word he rose and left the room, slipping ghost-like out the bedroom doorway.

I laid back down, brought my knees up to my chest, and pulled the covers around me.

# 16

I woke up early. For a moment, the previous night's events lay apart from my consciousness; then I sat up with a jerk, and ran downstairs. Leslie was still at home, and she reassured me that everyone was okay. She had seen Maggie and Emil, and Malissa, and was fairly certain that Mark had spent the night in Huntington Beach. Leslie didn't know about the other TC, but if something had happened to them, she was sure Malissa would have been told. With my immediate worries eased, I dressed and left for work at Slash.

Throughout the morning I remained preoccupied with the shooting. What the hell was going on? Was somebody actually hunting down punk rockers? And what about *tonight?* Would it happen again tonight?

It didn't take long for Robyn to realize that something was very wrong, and in response to her gentle prodding I poured out the whole horrific story. She listened with disbelief and concern, then immediately reached for her Rolodex. Opening it to a particular card, Robyn instructed me to call the man listed there; she assured me if I needed information, he was the person to talk to.

I dialed the number. The man who answered had not heard anything about punk rockers getting shot, but he promised that he would do some checking and get back to me. I thanked him and hung up. The rest of the day continued uneventfully.

It was late afternoon, and the light streaming into Biggs' office had grown dimmer. Suddenly the light was blocked entirely, as Biggs' tall figure loomed in the doorway. Behind him to his left was Slash's accountant, a small, balding man with bright eyes; to his right was John Doe. Biggs glared at me, his anger barely contained; he had just gotten off the phone with his wife, Penelope Spheeris, and she was not happy.

Penelope was a filmmaker. Earlier in the year she had filmed and conducted interviews with many of the local punk bands; that documentary, entitled The Decline of Western Civilization, was set to premiere in just a few days. That would be a tense time for any new director, and frayed nerves were understandable. So when a reporter called her to get her reaction to the shooting of a punk rocker, she apparently was... well, not happy.

Biggs wanted answers, and he wanted them now. I called L.A. Weekly? What was I thinking? Didn't I realize that negative publicity about punks and violence could adversely affect the success of Penelope's movie? Who did I think I was, to even be calling a reporter? The accusations came quickly, and I froze. I glanced at the accountant, and then at John Doe; John's eyes were alive, and there was a half-smile on his face. My God, I thought, he's enjoying this.

"Well?" My attention snapped back to Biggs. He was waiting for a response. I was aware of Robyn behind me; she moved slightly, but said nothing. Disgusted, Biggs pushed past me, followed by Doe. The accountant went back into his office. I sank into my chair.

A short time later Robyn approached me. In a hushed voice, she explained that she had been in trouble with Biggs lately, and if he knew of her responsibility in this matter, she'd be fired. She begged me to understand, and promised me she'd talk to Biggs, calm him down. She'd also make sure that I wouldn't lose my job. I nodded. I still had not spoken.

That night I sat outside on the porch overhang with Leslie, and disclosed the whole wretched mess. I didn't know what to do. My thoughts kept returning to Penelope, and Biggs - not to the questions they had, but to the ones they didn't. 'Are you all right?' 'Were any of your friends hurt?' 'Do you think someone is after punk rockers?', and 'How can we help?' Those questions would always lay unasked.

Leslie shook her head in disgust.

"So what are you going to do? Quit?" She didn't wait for a reply. "I would."

Leave Slash? But I didn't want to leave! I loved my job, despite what happened.

"Maybe it won't be up to you. Are you sure Robyn will talk to him?"

My hurt over the unfairness of the attack now plummeted into despair. Right about then, I wasn't sure of anything.

In the end there was no need to worry. Robyn did her part and spoke with Biggs; the incident was never mentioned again. But something inside me changed that day, because I never looked at Biggs in the same light again. In a strange way, I think I grew up a little.

As the days went by, things returned to normal - no more shootings were reported, and Penelope's movie debuted, as scheduled. It got great reviews.

# 17

It was one of the rare quiet evenings in the house, and I was in my bedroom. The night was very warm; my window was open, and through it came the sound of wheels crunching on pavement as Emil skated in front of the house. I dropped my spare pair of jeans on their spot on the floor, and went downstairs. The only other person in the house was Maggie; she was laying on her back with her eyes closed, listening to her Walkman.

Emil yelled to Maggie from outside, but lost in the music, she didn't hear him. Probably the Germs. I went over and shook her arm gently; she opened her eyes and removed her earphones. A complex composition of Mozart darted out, high and tinny, from the cheap Walkman. Classical music? But on second thought, it figured. Maggie was one of the few people who could still surprise me.

As she rose to answer Emil she suddenly cried out. Both hands clasped her stomach.

"What is it? What's wrong?"

Maggie didn't answer, she just shook her head, but her face clearly reflected her pain. Fifteen minutes later, the three of us were on our way to the emergency room.

We were lucky. It was also a quiet night at the hospital, and Maggie was seen almost right away. The doctor assured us that he wasn't too worried, but he wanted to run some tests nonetheless. Emil and I settled into our seats in the near-empty waiting room. The room was silent except for the water fountain. Every few moments the fountain's engine would snap on, the metal would rattle and buzz, and then silence would return. This went on for twenty minutes - click, buzz, silence. That water fountain had a rhythm all its own. It was very... what's the word? Pacific. I closed my eyes.

I must have dozed off for awhile, because the next thing I was aware of was the swish of the emergency room doors as they slid open, and the peacefulness around us vanished.

Three young men stormed in. I recognized the type: skinny, long greasy hair, holey jeans, black t-shirts. Heavy metal. One of them was holding up his hand, and cursing loudly. The nurse hurried around and escorted him to the back, while his two companions grabbed the requisite forms and sat down to write. Emil's expression changed; he was watching them sort of like a mouse watches a circling hawk.

The taller one spotted Emil. Already bored with the form, he tossed the pen down and raised his eyebrows.

"What are you looking at?"

Emil didn't reply, reaching instead for a magazine. That wasn't good enough for the young man, who was sniffing out a new form of amusement. He elbowed his companion, nodding in our direction; he then said something under his breath, and they both laughed. His eyes never left Emil.

"Fucking punks."

It was barely loud enough for us to hear. When we didn't respond, he tried again.

"What should we do about these fucking punks?"

Okay, we heard that. I couldn't believe it. We were going to get jumped, right there in the emergency room. I mean, it's not like we could run for it; there was no way we were leaving Maggie. The leather sleeve of the shorter boy rode up, revealing a sculpted bicep. Just our luck - we found the only heavy metal fan with a muscle.

Emil closed the magazine, and without a word he walked casually into the hallway. The young man watched him intently, just waiting for that sudden move to trigger him into action. From where I sat I could see a payphone on the wall; Emil put a dime in, and began to speak quietly into the receiver. The other two probably couldn't see him, but they didn't appear too worried. There was just the one door - and besides, they still had me.

Emil came back in and took the seat next to me.

"Emil," I whispered hoarsely, "what do we do?"

No response. I glanced at him; his eyes were closed. Oh, shit. Oh, shit. My heart began to race; could they hear it? The tall one stood up... Then the emergency door slid open, and there was a streak of black leather...

Shirley came around the corner. And Jason. And Animal. And a couple of more Hollywood punks from around town. Emil's eyes were still closed, but now he was smiling. Great boy!

I glanced over triumphantly at our would-be attackers; the taller one had literally shrank back onto the plastic chair. It gave a little squeak. Without even a glimpse in the metal boys' direction, Shirley approached us.

"You guys having some trouble?" she asked in a loud voice.

Jason, all 6 feet 200 pounds of him, towered in front of us. They were beautiful.

Shortly afterwards, Maggie was released from the emergency room and sent home. She was fine. And because of friends, and a ten cent phone call, so was I.

# 18

March rolled around, and with it, my birthday. I learned that Maggie and I were born on the same day, a discovery that further cemented our friendship.

It was close to five o'clock. Biggs was in his office with Exene and John Doe, and I was finishing up the last of my work. Suddenly there were loud voices in the stairwell, and the TC poured into the waiting room! Maggie was there, and Emil, and Malissa - even Pat Smear of The Germs had showed up to help me celebrate. I never did ask permission to stop work, but really, what choice did I have? The office was filled now with laughter and jesting and horseplay, so I did the only logical thing possible. I wallowed in it.

In the midst of all this I felt a hand on my shoulder. It was Exene. Her black-lined eyes flashed, and her crimson lips pulled back into a smile. I realized that I had never seen her smile before. It was a little unnerving.

"It's your birthday?" she declared in a loud, theatrical voice. "Well, *happy birthday!*"

She wrapped her arms around me - with her black clothing and jangling bracelets, it was sort of like being enveloped by a large, noisy crow. I thanked her awkwardly, and at the same time tried to hide my confusion. Exene was talking - to me? During the past few months, she had stopped to chat and gossip with Biggs, and Robyn, and even the accountant... but never with me. I supposed that she could be making an exception for my birthday, but still...

As Exene continued to stand there and smile at me, I slowly became aware of the other faces in the room. Malissa. Maggie. Pat Smear. They had been on the scene a long time; they knew of Exene. Or, more to the point, she knew of them. Was this why she was being so nice? Not because of me... but because of them?

And then it occurred to me that maybe that was why Exene never spoke to me, or even acknowledged my existance; maybe she didn't want to be liked just for being the singer of X, any more than I wanted to be liked for having the right friends. Maybe she had embraced this moment as a chance to share that enlightenment with me. Maybe she was trying to teach me a very special lesson, one that I would take with me throughout my life...

Nah.

When I got home that night, the kids gave me homemade birthday cards. They were plainly drawn, with simple expressions of affection. I knew then that I wouldn't trade the TC for all the celebrities in the world.

Maggie

Emil

Malissa and Brian

Bobbi

Mark

Judy

Gloria

Joni

Critter

Leslie

Petey's dashboard

Ricky

The Oziehares play the Starwood

Mark and Lane on stage

Gloria and Stephanie whoop it up in
the Tower Records parking lot

Gloria, wearing the infamous sticker

Adam Ant, looking nervous

The L.A. Weekly cover

-used by permission Mark Vallen

Maggie

Amie

# 19

There was a new punk in town. His name was Ray. Tall and strapping, with dark, heavy good looks, Ray had recently been featured in a documentary called Rude Boy; the film followed the misadventures of a roadie for the rock band The Clash. Rachel discovered the young Brit at a local party, and one night she brought him back to the house.

Ray had a unique ability. He could use the f-word in more situations and expressions than anyone I had ever met. He used it as an adverb, an adjective, an exclamation; under Ray's tutelage, the f-word became a conjunction, and a preposition, and even a punctuation mark. It signalled his anger and rage; it also spoke for his joy, hope, sympathy, and love. He put a significant amount of energy into finding new ways to share it with us. Ray could dice, splice, scramble, broil, bake, and fry that word. He was a master chef of profanity.

Ray was going to a party in the Valley, and he offered Maggie a lift. Out of malice, or simple neglect, he later left her, and returned to the house alone. Maggie called a short while before he arrived; she was stuck out there, with no way to get back. As Malissa worked on arrangements to bring Maggie home, I grew more and more angry at Ray. He had no excuse for leaving her stranded, especially in the Valley. That was not our home turf, and finding yourself on your own there could quickly turn dangerous if you ran into a drunk jock with a bone to pick.

When Ray finally wandered in, a vacant smile on his face, I lost my temper. Or rather, I felt like I *should* lose my temper, so I marched right up to him and demanded to know why he had abandoned Maggie. Ray, looking as if I had asked him to point out Uruguay on a map, merely shrugged. I wanted to slap him. I knew I should slap him. Unfortunately, I had never hit a guy, and I hesitated. For a good five seconds we just stared at each other - I working up the courage to strike him, and Ray wondering what he should have for dinner. Then I opened my hand, and hit him across the face. It was not a very hard hit; the soft sound of skin against skin was barely audible. He looked surprised, I'm sure no more so than I. Ray shrugged again.

"Fuck," he offered.

I couldn't have said it better myself.

# 20

My car was the coolest. A yellow Datsun B-210, it was bright and cheerful. And though it never ripped on the sides of a pool, or edged along the perimeter of a schoolyard, it had another, better skill. It flew.

Los Angeles streets were created with dips. I'm not sure what they were for - to catch water from the rare rainstorm, or perhaps to slow down a speeding driver. Whatever its designers' intent, its true purpose was to give a car wings. We would approach an intersection and there the dip would be. Waiting. Beckoning. My foot would hit the gas, and the little car would come at the dip with the skill of a primed palomino approaching a six foot gate. Steady.... steady... the slightest hesitation and then... a leap. A gleeful second suspended in air, then the return of rubber to pavement, a dangerous sideways swerve, and straight again. It was a wonder to see.

Of course, it wasn't nearly so fun for passengers in the back seat. Just ask Maggie. We were approaching an intersection, and she recognized that sparkle in my eye.

"Amie..." she warned.

Too late. She raised her arms to brace herself, the car lifted up... and over! Good car! As I affectionately patted its dashboard, Maggie cursed, rubbing the top of her hair.

"Damn it, Amie!" She leaned over and smacked me in the

head, but it was a playful slap.

The next time my car came through for me, the situation was a little more serious.

Emil needed a ride to Santa Monica, to meet some guy, or something. I made the turn down a quiet, tree-lined street and pulled up in front of a small apartment building. Emil told me to stay put, he'd be right back. As he disappeared into the building I reached over and put a cassette tape in the player. I was going through my James Bond phase at the moment, which explained why the theme to 'Goldfinger' suddenly filled my car.

It probably sounds silly, but I wanted to be a spy so bad! Earlier that year I had even contacted the CIA. They had an office in Lawndale, and I sent them my application. I wasn't sure what work they would offer me ... typing letters probably. But that would be a waste, in my opinion; after all, I'd make the perfect cover. With my hair and clothes, who would ever suspect that I was a secret agent? Unfortunately, the CIA saw it differently, because they turned me down flat. Something about having enough spies at the moment...

'Dawn Raid on Fort Knox' was just beginning on the cassette player when the passenger door flew open.

"Go!" Emil's voice was commanding, but his eyes were wide and terrified.

"Emil, what are you doing? What's wrong?"

"Just go! Go! Amie, *go!*"

When I didn't react fast enough, Emil tried to grab the gear shift himself. Annoyed, I pushed his arm away.

"Emil, what the..."

There was a movement in the rear-view mirror. A girl, some-one I had never seen before, was about ten yards away. She was walking towards the car, slowly, almost as if she was in a daze. Suddenly a man ran up behind her and grabbed her, one arm around her waist, the other hand sliding across her mouth. Emil saw this too, and when he turned back to me, his eyes were pleading. My foot slammed onto the gas.

The Datsun lurched forward, gained speed, and took off. I didn't look back. A stop sign was ahead. We blew right through it. A skid, but control was regained. Down one block, and a right. Another harder right. Now left. A dip loomed ahead of us, but my car did not hesitate. It took us right over. Emil hit the window as we landed, but we kept going.

"Here! Turn in here!" He was pointing to an alley. I pulled in and hit the brakes.

"It's okay. It's okay now." Emil may have been talking to me, but I wasn't sure. He opened the door.

"It's okay. Just wait here."

It's okay... it's okay... I was comforting myself now. Whatever the danger was, we had escaped. I allowed myself to exhale, and take a few slower, deeper breaths. The Bond music had ended; the tape was rewinding. I patted the dashboard. It was okay...

I never learned who the girl was, why the man had grabbed her, or what Emil was doing there in the first place. But I did know one thing.

The CIA had their chance. They blew it.

# 21

April 11, 1981. The day Adam Ant came to town.

Adam and the Ants were a British group - one of the many New Wave bands who came to Los Angeles to play their music, make their deals, and sell more records. During a recent interview a reporter incorrectly described the Ants as a punk band, a label that did not sit well with Adam. He responded in the press with an attack on punk rock in general, and punk rockers in particular.

That was a mistake.

A local radio station had scheduled Adam and the Ants to appear at Tower Records on Sunset. A couple of hours before the band was supposed to show up, Critter appeared at the house with a handful of stickers, about the size of four inch squares. On the stark white background were black letters that proclaimed Black Flag Kills Ants On Contact. With those stickers, a carton of eggs in our camera case, and a gleam in our mischievous little eyes, we were ready to welcome Adam and the Ants to America.

As we shut the front door behind us, my eye caught that movement again - the face darting back from the window, the swing of the curtain on its rod. Damn it. There she was again... I glared across the street. What was wrong with her? Why couldn't she mind her own business? If the landlady came, and she told her about...

My thoughts were interrupted by Petey's van, which clipped

our curb as it squealed to a stop. I loved that old van; it had a broken windshield, and 'Sex Pistols' was written on the dashboard in masking tape. After one more resentful glance at the neighbor, I piled into the vehicle with the rest of the TC.

As the van pulled away from the house, my mood lifted. The cheerful old Beatles song 'Baby You Can Drive My Car' was cranking out from the speakers. All the girls were wearing similar outfits - white shirt, straight leg blue jeans, suspenders, and biker boots. We were dressed for bear, determined to make a unified statement; at the very least, we were not going to be confused with the Ant followers.

Say what you will about them, Adam's fans were unique. They dressed up in feathers and old band uniforms, creating a look that fell somewhere between an Apache and a movie usher. When we arrived they were already crowding the parking lot in front of Tower Records. We took the area by storm.

As Ant music blared in blissful ignorance on enormous speakers, Stephanie and Gloria whooped and danced like Indians, easily clearing a wide circle in the crowd. The Ant followers bunched into little piles, well away from us. I'm not sure whether it was the dancing that sent them scurrying, or the Black Flag Kills Ants On Contact stickers. In actuality, we had nothing against the Ant fans; we were simply in high spirits and getting a little punchy as we waited for Adam to appear. It didn't take much longer.

There was a scream, and then a chorus of screams, as Adam Ant made his way onto the stage. Adam was actually quite handsome, with that dark wavy hair and smooth white skin, and he did have a good voice. Under other circumstances, I might have enjoyed hearing him sing. But this was war.

I peered up at the top of the bluff overlooking the parking lot, and was just able to make out Maggie's black dreadlocks. They were in position; we were ready. I was waiting in line for the honor of asking the pop star a question. The girl directly in front of me grabbed Adam roughly by the back of the neck and kissed him.

Now it was my turn; as the impatient crowd pushed me ahead, Adam looked down at me with amused expectation. I raised my voice above the screams.

"Adam... what do you think of punk rock?"

He glanced away, dismissively.

"I don't think about punk rock," Adam replied. "I only think about Ant music."

All... righty-roo.

I backed away from the stage. Adam stood up, took his place in front of the microphone... and was greeted with a hail of eggs. Those kids had great aim. Angry promoters started yelling, burly bouncers started chugging up the hill, and, though there was only one volley of eggs, Adam spent much of the next twenty minutes glancing uneasily, and repeatedly, at the top of the cliff. Eventually he resolved that becoming an omelet wasn't in his contract; he packed it up, and we returned home, triumphant. The whole episode was more than a little silly, but it was also a welcome relief, especially for kids branded 'this violent generation'.

Later that afternoon Ricky came tearing into the house with urgent news: the landlady was driving up! Kids flew out the back door, out the windows, over the schoolyard fence... so by the time Mrs. Mangold reached the front porch, I was innocently alone. As I opened the door, she peered past me into the living room, her eye sharp for discrepancies.

"Miss Cooper... I've been told that there are more than two people living here... is that true?" I've never been a good liar, but standing on that front porch, I lied my head off anyway.

"No, Mrs. Mangold, I don't know what you mean. It's just me and Leslie here."

She pressed her lips together and nodded, but in a manner that told me she didn't believe me for a second. Legally, though, there wasn't much she could do. She had to catch us at it first.

As her car slowly drew away from the curb, I looked across the street. The curtain fell back into place.

# 22

Well, if it was adventure and danger that I wanted, then the evening of April 15 was shaping up to be just the ticket. That's because that night found me in the back seat of my B-210, on the way to a rumble.

The TC were in two cars heading straight for Oki Dog, the small hamburger stand on Santa Monica Boulevard that had become a popular hangout for Hollywood punks. Apparently somebody had said something or done something to somebody else, and we were all to meet him and his friends in Oki Dog's parking lot.

As the street signs flew past my window, I thought to myself "Gee. I'm on my way to a rumble." I wasn't quite sure what to do. Since I had never hit anyone before (with the exception of Ray's slap), I wasn't sure when the time came that I could actually do it. And what about being on the receiving end of a fist, or a boot, or a pipe? Wouldn't that hurt - like, a lot?

On the other hand, the idea of a rumble sounded kind of cool and dangerous. There had been a passage in The Outsiders where Ponyboy got jumped, and it sure made a black eye sound tuff. From the look of it, tonight would be an excellent opportunity to get one for my very own.

We reached the corner on Santa Monica where Oki Dog sat, and both cars whipped into the parking lot. There was no one there. Unsure whether our quarry had chickened out or was merely late, one carful of kids went out hunting for them; I stayed behind, along with a couple of the boys.

Not five minutes had gone by when one of the TC kids got in a verbal sparring match with a heavy-set Hispanic man. They cussed back and forth at each other for a minute, while I look nervously about for reinforcements; then he shoved my friend, and all my apprehension disappeared. I charged the man.

Like a giant bothered by a pesky flake of dandruff, he reached over and flicked me off of him. The next thing I knew I was lying on my back, looking up at the sky. I remember thinking, "I'm lying on my back, looking up at the sky."

Our adversaries never did show up. No rumble. No black eye.

At least the hamburgers were good.

# 23

Okay, pop quiz. How many punks can you fit in a Datsun B-210? (No, it's not a trick question.) The answer is nine. At least, that's how many we squeezed in for our trip down to Mexico.

Emil had heard that the surf was huge down in Baja, and he talked eight of us into joining him - the boys for the waves, and the girls for the shopping. I'd been to Mexico before, with my parents, but we went to the usual places that would interest tourists - Cozumel, Chichén Itzá, Mexico City. We stayed at the nicest hotels. There would be no nice hotels this time.

We drove all the way without stopping; the answer to 'Are we there yet?' was given when the boys spotted a big enough wave. As the guys unleashed the boards from the roof of my car, pulling out wet suits and cords and the round, colorful bars of Sex Wax, the girls walked towards the small, cone-shaped huts that dotted the beach. These provided cover for the beach-goer who was spending the night and didn't want to be exposed to the night breeze.

I peered into one of the huts. It was dark inside, cramped and cool. What little light there was had to come through the cracks in the thatched material, but it was enough to discern movement. Make that *movements*. Multitudes of some very large bug went scurrying across the walls - I had no idea what kind of insect it was, but I wasn't waiting around to find out. Besides, I liked the night breeze.

Maggie, Rachel and Stephanie were sitting under a palm tree, gossiping. I kept my distance. Separately, we got on great with each other - but when those girls were a threesome they became boisterous and cocksure, a little like the intimidating cliques of high school. Their loud voices only served to stir up my shyness and old insecurities.

I walked back to the boys. Munskie was pulling on his wetsuit. He shook his curls as they emerged from the rubber suit, and his eyes were pure happiness as he scanned the sea. Munskie was rather sweet, and kind, with a slight build and gentle, handsome face. He lived in Santa Monica, and only occasionally visited us in Hollywood. A true surfer, his greatest joys came when he was in the water; anything on shore could only place second.

Despite rumors of shark sightings in the area, he and Emil slid their boards into the foaming surf without a hint of trepidation. Boys being boys, they weren't about to let a bite or two keep them from the best waves they'd seen in a while. I, on the other hand, liked having ten fingers and ten toes, so I turned my back on the inviting sea, and strolled into the nearby town.

Exploring all on my own came naturally to me. My favorite part was allowing myself to get lost - to wander up unmarked lanes, or dart into exotic shops. And *foreign* countries - why, they were an adventure just waiting to happen!

I remembered some Spanish from high school, enough to heighten the enjoyment of interacting with the shopkeepers. As the sun beat down on my face, I passed ice cream carts and out-door cafes, their tables littered with half-empty bottles of water and Coca-Cola. The storefronts were splashes of bright colors, all reds and oranges and lime greens. Heaven.

After a couple of hours of perusing the local streets, I went back to the beach. It was starting to get late, and the boys were just coming out of the ocean; they had apparently managed to surf without losing any body parts. As night fell we ate some tortillas that Emil was able to scrounge, and everyone hit the sack - er, sand. The long drive, the sun, and the salty air had taken its toll, and it wasn't long before we were asleep.

The next day we all went into town for some shopping and exploring. Most of the items in the shops were very affordable, and even the tortillas sold for only five cents. The boys stocked up on them for the long trip back.

Maggie and I went into a sort of gift shop, and while I browsed in the back, she approached the storekeepers; they were an older Mexican couple, perhaps in their fifties.

"Um, Señor? Yeah, you. Hola. Cuantos... is this shit?"

That appeared to be the extent of her Spanish. The Mexican frowned and shook his head, and she tried again. I began to make my way to the front of the store, but by then Maggie's frustration was getting the better of her. Her voice became increasingly loud, as the pace of it slowed... significantly. The effect was shockingly rude.

The shopkeeper's eyes grew angry, but at the same time he appeared resigned, as if he had been through this same kind of conversation, and more than once. Maggie finally gave up, dancing lightly through the sunlit doorway. The man glanced at me and I shrugged, apologetically, then gave him my best smile. It was not returned.

We caught up to the rest of the gang, just in time for my second chance at a rumble. The boys had apparently managed to piss off a couple of local young roosters, who appeared more than eager to give them a fight. I walked to within a few feet of one of the men. The sun was shining in my face, and my head was roaring, perhaps from the contrast between this street and the cool, dark shop.

I never saw the man's movement, for the next thing I knew Munskie had grabbed me roughly and pulled me behind him. At the same time his hand went to his pocket; there was a flash of metal from under his palm as the knife reflected the sun. Time seemed to freeze, and a second slipped into moments. Suddenly, a shout rang out from further down the street - I made out the word 'Federales'; it was then repeated, with more urgency. The man in front of me hesitated, then cursed, and ran off; we took off as well, in the opposite direction. It was definitely time to go home.

As we got back into the car for the drive back, I reflected on what had happened, and nearly happened. With his brave action, Munskie had unwittingly stepped into the leading role of every gothic novel I had ever read. He had yanked me back from the brink of danger - and in a foreign land, no less! It was without a doubt the single most romantic thing that had ever happened to me.

I turned to gaze at my heroic rescuer, only to find he had nodded off, mouth slightly open, a low snore emanating from his lips. I didn't remember *that* happening in any novel...

I smiled to myself. Oh, well. It wasn't exactly a white horse... but it would do.

# 24

Girls have a lot of difficulty saying no. Have you ever noticed that? It's like it's wired into us to be as helpful and accommodating as possible, even when it's to our disadvantage. We get into a lot of trouble that way. Anyway, that's how I got myself into a lot of trouble.

It seemed harmless enough. Emil wanted to borrow the car for a while. Just for a little while. When a fifteen-year-old boy who has no driver's license, little driving experience, and who really needs to be home doing something sensible, like, say, SLEEPING, wants to borrow your car... well, you pretty much know what the answer should be. I *knew* that I should say no, perhaps with a roll of my eyes thrown in for good measure. And so when Emil asked to borrow my car, I responded... "Yeah. Okay. Sure, go ahead." I think I may even have added "Have a good time!"

Maggie, on the other hand, never had a problem speaking her mind, and when she learned that I had lent my car to Emil, I found myself in the ridiculous position of being lectured to by someone younger than myself. If that didn't make me feel stupid enough, I couldn't even explain to her why I had done it. There was nothing I could say to Maggie, but there was something I could do; I could find Emil, and my car, and bring them both back home.

I caught a ride to Oki Dog, figuring it was my best bet for tracking down Emil; after all, sooner or later, everyone ended up there.

But the hamburger stand was surprisingly quiet. Only a few kids were there, and none of them Emil. I made the rounds of the picnic tables, but no one had seen him that night. There was nothing left to do but wait.

An hour went by, and then another, and still no sign of Emil. On top of that, there was work tomorrow. I told myself that Emil was probably back home. I told myself that I didn't have a choice, that this was just wasting time. I told myself it was time to go home. There was just one small problem. My ride had taken off an hour earlier, and none of the kids remaining were ready to go just yet. So it was left for me to fall back on an old pleasure of mine - hitchhiking.

My first year of college I hitched everywhere. I thumbed my way up to San Francisco, and caught rides in convertibles down Sunset Strip. The freedom was wonderful. I was too young and inexperienced, of course, to know how stupid it was. So once again I didn't hesitate. I put out my thumb.

At 11 p.m. there was little traffic on the street, and it was starting to look like I might be there all evening... Suddenly lights appeared, and a car swerved towards me. But it wasn't a ride. It was the police.

The cop leaned out of the passenger side.

"When we come back here, I want you to be gone."

That was it. No words of concern, no offer to help. As a punk rocker, I probably shouldn't have expected a friendly response - to be honest, we had pretty much used up our goodwill. The car pulled away. I now found myself with a Catch-22. They clearly didn't want me hitchhiking anymore, but if they also wanted me 'gone', the only way I was going to get gone was to hitchhike. I looked around cautiously, and again stuck out my thumb.

I swear, they must have set a speed record going around that corner. The police car plowed into the parking lot; the brakes squealed and both cops jumped out, one in front of me, the other behind.

"Let's see some ID." I shook my head, confused and a little frightened by all the fuss.

"I don't have any..."

A pair of handcuffs were clamped onto my wrists before the sentence could be completed. My gosh, was this really happening? Frantically scanning the patrons of Oki Dog for any friendly face, I yelled "Tell Maggie!" to no one in particular. If they heard me they gave no sign. The policeman put me in the back seat of the squad car, and pulled away.

I was under arrest.

The cops didn't say one word to me all the way to the precinct. After my initial fear subsided, I looked around the back seat with curiosity. This was my first time in the back of a police car. There was something I had always been curious about, from all those years of watching police dramas on television... wasn't there a way to slip out from handcuffs? I doubted the police would share it with me if there was, so it was up to me to find out. I put my fingers together, and tried to squeeze out my hand. No go. I tried sitting on my hands and bringing my knees up to my chin. Not a chance. Then I flopped over on my side, pushed down with my hands, and tried to get one leg between my arms. All the while I was turning myself into a pretzel, the cops said nothing. I guess they already knew all about handcuffs.

Eventually we reached the station, going in the back way. With one hand on my shoulder, the officer led me to a chair. He sat across from me and began to type on a form, while his partner leaned against a nearby desk, studying me. Along with the basic questions of name and address and stuff like that, came rude, unprofessional comments about my hair and my clothes and my general appearance. After a few minutes of this with no reaction, the partner grew tired of the sport; he stopped trying to bait me, they finished the paperwork, and I was sent down the line.

Next up was the picture taking - I mean, the mug shot. The cop in charge of this area was a big, older man. Following his direction, I stepped up on a platform and turned to face the camera. When it became clear he was going to take my picture, I smiled. He looked up, startled.

"You're not supposed to smile."

Oh. Right. I furrowed my brow in an attempt to look as mean as possible. The shutter clicked.

"Turn to the left."

Was there a tinge of amusement in his voice? Once again, I scowled for the camera.

Now it was fingerprint time. The officer pressed my thumb down onto the ink blotter, then moved it to a piece of paper. I squinted down at the imprint. Now *that* was interesting. As I bent down closer to peer at the swirling marks, I put my dyed thumb parallel to the print, and tried to match up the lines. The policeman cleared his throat, and I straightened up. It wasn't my imagination; he was amused. I was beginning to feel like the evening's entertainment.

Next he extended a bucket in front of me.

"You put your hand in there to get the ink off," he advised helpfully.

Dipping a finger daintily into the goop, I drew out a dime-sized piece and rubbed it between my fingers. His mouth quivered as he tried, and failed, to prevent a grin.

"It's okay, just dunk your whole hand in there. Go ahead, it's all right."

I got some more of the goop, accepted the paper towels he handed me, and cleaned my hands. I was sorry to have to leave him. He was nice.

On to the holding area. There was a pay phone on the wall; they gave me the opportunity to make one phone call. I called home, but nothing happened; it didn't even ring. I couldn't understand it - why was there no ringing? Then I remembered Disaster. Disaster was a large white and tan rabbit that I had bought recently; besides leaving pellets everywhere, he chewed on everything.

He chewed on the stairs - he chewed on the wall - he chewed on the phone line... He chewed on the phone line.

*He chewed on the phone line.*

My one phone call had been wasted. Dismayed and exhausted, I sat down on a nearby bench. It was smooth and hard. I curled up on the bench and closed my eyes; its surface felt cool against my cheek. After a little while another woman was put into the holding area with me; she was a youngish black woman dressed like a prostitute. As a woman police officer passed by, my new roommate started shouting "I didn't do nuthin'! I didn't do *nuthin*!" She glanced at me for validation, and I shrugged. I guess she didn't do nuthin'.

A couple of minutes of yelling later a male officer walked up. He was clearly not as patient as the other cop, and it only took another minute of the prostitute's loud protests before he slammed his fist down on the counter. I went to the woman and led her, still protesting, to an empty bench, then returned to my own bench and laid down once again. The female officer gestured towards me.

"See? Why can't you be more like her?"

After about an hour I was transferred to my own cell. It wasn't anything like I imagined it would be. Where were the cell bars that jails always have in the movies? This was a solid white room, quite spartan; there was one set of bunk beds against the wall, and a single narrow, vertical window in the door that looked out into a bare hallway. Though I'm sure the room was meant to be calming, it possessed a smothering, almost claustrophobic aura. Ironically, the next ten hours were the worst for me. They likely put me in there by myself to protect me from the other prisoners, but with no one to talk to, I began to feel isolated and a little scared. I lay down and closed my eyes.

I woke up disoriented. I didn't know what time it was, or even what day it was. It was an awful sensation. There was no one in the hallway, and when I banged on the window to get someone's attention, the noise evaporated in a muffled thud. Turning my back on the door, I took a deep breath. Stay calm. Just stay calm. I then took hold of the vertical stand supporting the bunk beds, and did what any incarcerated prisoner would do in my situation. I did my ballet exercises. One and two and three and - plié! It made me feel a little better.

Eventually the door to my cell opened, and an officer escorted me to the bail area. Leslie was there, waiting for me. She had paid my fine - all ten dollars of it. We picked up my little bits of property and left.

Leslie pulled up across from the house; my wayward car was right out front, sitting sheepishly by the curb. A couple of the kids were in the kitchen making breakfast; they offered me some, but I was much too tired to eat. Instead I went upstairs and flopped down on my bed, relishing how wonderful it was to be in my own room.

I had been lying there awhile, listening to the yells of the children playing in the schoolyard, when I realized that I had forgotten to ask the officer what the charge had been. The fine was only ten dollars, after all, so it couldn't have been too serious. What was it - hitchhiking? Loitering? Or - maybe just... being a punk rocker?

We should find out. I could probably call and find out... later.

I drifted off to sleep.

# 25

May approached, and with it the promise of a warm summer and weeks of fun. It would also see our life at St. Andrews Place come to an abrupt end.

Work was over for the day, and as the car turned onto our street, I was thinking about nothing more important than our plans for the weekend. Suddenly it felt like there was a hand closing over my throat. Mrs. Mangold's car was parked in front of the house, and Mrs. Mangold herself was standing on our porch. She glanced stonily at me as I pulled up behind her car. There were ten or so kids milling around. Their presence told Mrs. Mangold what she needed to know; the distress on their faces told me what I needed to know. Mrs. Mangold left the porch to greet me. I searched her face for a look of triumph, but there wasn't any, really. She was simply matter-of-fact.

We had two weeks to leave.

Leslie and I found another house to move to almost right away, but this time around there would be no subterfuge, because this time we would be moving en masse. The TC were coming with us.

I returned to St. Andrews one last time to get the security deposit back from Mrs. Mangold. She gave me a fair amount, then eyed me curiously and inquired where we would be going next.

The last thing I wanted to do right about then was engage in a pleasant chat with my soon-to-be ex-landlady, and wished only that she would go away. Mrs. Mangold must have sensed my feelings, because she shrugged, and drove off.

I took a last look at that house, the one that meant so much to all of us, before returning to my car. It was then that I noticed the woman crossing the street towards me. She was middle-aged, pale, with delicate skin. Her voice was low and weak.

"Are you leaving?"

I wasn't sure I had heard her correctly. She came closer.

"Are you leaving?"

It was then that I realized who it was - it was our neighbor, the one from across the street. The spy.

My back stiffened. She was the one who got us kicked out of our wonderful home. Well, if she had come to gloat, she was wasting her time. I wouldn't give her the satisfaction.

"Yes, we're moving." My voice was hard, but I did try to keep the sarcasm out of it.

"Oh." It was barely above a whisper. She looked over at the old house, then back at me. "I'm sorry."

Yeah, I bet. How long was this going to take?

"I'm sorry... to see you go." She was looking straight at me. Her eyes were a light blue, clear and gentle, without a hint of disingenuousness. I shook my head, confused. "You're... sorry to see us go?" I repeated.

She nodded solemnly, but with a touch of a smile.

"You brought so much life to the block."

I didn't know what to say. She turned, her shoulders slightly bent, crossed the street, and went back inside her home. This time, the curtain was still.

# 26

The Oxford House. If the home on St. Andrews Place radiated warmth and family, the Oxford House was built on a psychic fault line. This new place was bigger, with larger rooms and more of them. The owners had converted the attic, as well, thus giving the house a total of five bedrooms. At first we were excited about all the extra space - it meant privacy in bedrooms, less waiting for bathrooms, and no more stacking up on the living room floor. But when the physical closeness that St. Andrews necessitated was gone, much of the emotional closeness we had shared seemed to go with it.

Our neighbors were also very different. On two sides were older Korean immigrants, who from the very first day watched us (not surprisingly) with suspicion and fear. Not long after moving in my rabbit Disaster disappeared. I had left him outside in our backyard, in a fenced pen; it would give him a chance to eat something other than telephone cords, and also be able to enjoy the sun and fresh air. When I went to check on him and he was gone, I couldn't figure out how he got out. There were no holes either in or under the fencing that would have provided an escape route.

A couple of days later I asked one of the young Korean boys next door if they had seen my rabbit. He nonchalantly acknowledged that he had. They had caught Disaster two nights earlier, and eaten him for dinner. The boy seemed surprised by the expression on my face.

Across the street was an older, two-story house, with a wood gingerbread design fringing the roof. The people in this house appeared to accept us, or if it wasn't exactly acceptance, they at least minded their own business. But there was something odd about them. There seemed to be an awful lot of strangers coming and going, and especially throughout the night. But the strangest thing about that house was the light; at night, every night, a red glow would appear from the upstairs window, turning the room an eerie shade of scarlet.

Curiosity finally got the better of Maggie and me. One cloudy afternoon we went up to the house to introduce ourselves; a man wearing sunglasses opened the door, but only partially. As we attempted to peer in he lifted a hand in front of us to block our view, and strongly suggested that we return to our own home. Maggie tried her hardest to talk her way in, but in the end she had to concede defeat. It was only weeks later that we learned that it was, in actuality, a whore-house, one that specialized in domination.

For a short while, Black Flag came and stayed with us. They had recently been kicked out of their place in Torrance; their landlord had apparently failed to mention that, unlike gas and water, police harassment *was* included. Their bass player, Chuck, was good friends with Malissa, and it was she who suggested that Chuck and Greg speak to me about the possibility of their moving in, at least until they found a new house. Polite and ever-professional, Greg offered to pay fifty dollars a month in rent; when I jokingly suggested I would prefer five percent of their album profits, he shot back brightly that I'd be smarter to take the fifty bucks.

It was one of the few humorous moments we would have in our new home.

# 27

Maggie and Emil were going down to Long Beach, so I went with them. I had never been to the town, but the name was appealing. Long Beach. It created images of wide expanses of sand, overrun by white foam. But if Long Beach had a beach, I sure as hell couldn't find it.

There were rocky crags and cement pilings, not to mention one particularly odious, diesel-laden boat dock, but that wasn't in the plans. Where the heck was the beach? A native Long Beacher filling up his car's gas tank noticed my confusion, and he suggested checking out Seal Beach. He assured me it was clean, sandy, and close by. That sounded absolutely perfect. Since Emil and Maggie would be occupied most of the day, I went there by myself.

Seal Beach was everything the man said it was. It stretched out in front of me, bright and warm and beckoning. I made my way along the wide sidewalk that paralled the ocean, past the pastel-colored beach houses, until I reached the entrance. My heavy motorcycle boots sank into the sand as I trudged towards the water. I didn't have plans to go swimming, or anything like that; I just wanted to touch the water. There weren't many other people on the beach, but as it turned out, there were just enough.

I was less than halfway to the shore when a dozen or so young men and women surrounded me. They were all very blond and very tan - California's version of the 'beautiful' people. At first they had merely followed me, but their formation quickly solidified into a sort of a gauntlet. It *was* a gauntlet. And I was their prize.

The taunts started right away. It was the usual stuff - snipes about my hair, and my clothes. Nothing particularly original. While the girls just sounded catty, the boys' tone quickly began to worry me. There was an edge to it that told me that this was more than just some nasty fun for them... that this could really be danger.

The suddenness of the threat was so bizarre... especially when juxtaposed with the blue sky and the warm sun, and the volleyball nets. One of the boys was wearing swimtrunks dotted with happy, cartoon-like fish. The whole thing was surreal. For some reason that made it even scarier.

They didn't try to block me from leaving, but dogged me at an increasingly close pace. What did they want from me, damn it? Why couldn't these guys just leave me alone? If anyone else on the beach sensed my distress, they kept it to themselves. If I was to get out of this, I was to do so on my own.

Just as their cursing went up another notch, I broke away at a dead sprint. You would think that they would have expected such a move, but still they were caught off guard. By the time the boys gathered themselves, I had all the lead I needed. They weren't going to catch this ex co-captain of her track team. Not even in bulky, chain-wrapped boots! Reaching my car I slid into the driver's seat, peeled out, and in the rear-view mirror watched my tormentors steadily disappear.

In the car heading back home, Maggie asked about my visit to the beach. I had already decided not to tell them about the gauntlet; it would serve no purpose, and besides, I just wanted to forget it. But if I thought I could pull that off, I was kidding myself. Maggie had an innate perception when it came to reading her friends. She studied my face intently.

"Something happened, didn't it?" she demanded.

When I didn't respond, Maggie stated with certainty "I knew it."

Despite her continued prodding, however, I kept my secret.

I did manage to become injured a little later, but I had only myself to blame.

Maggie, Emil, and I had gone to a local park where a birthday party was being thrown for a friend's young son. While the guests devoured the cake and opened presents, I gazed at the grassy slope extending up the hill. I remembered what Tony had taught me - if you can imagine it, you can skate it. If I could imagine it...

Without any hesitation, or sense, I climbed the slope. Reaching the top, I began to skate down the slick grass. At first it was fun, and easy; as the board gathered speed, however, I began to lose my balance. The skateboard wobbled unsteadily beneath my feet; I tried to counter the movement but overcompensated, and it shot out from under my feet. Flying vertically into the air, I came down on my back. Hard.

Then the only thing I could imagine was pain.

Every breath brought sharp stabs into my side; by the time Maggie found me, the pain from my jerking sobs was excruciating. She flew back down the hill to get help. The next thing I knew, Tito was standing over me; he was a friend of Maggie's, and played in a local band called The Plugz.

Tito sat beside me on the grass, and began to tell me of a terrible car accident that he had witnessed. Both the story and his voice were an eerie echo of Ricky's midnight account of the shooting, but the intent was far different. As his story unfolded, his voice low and steady, I was as mesmorized as I was sickened. It was a truly terrible and personal event, the kind that mucks about in your soul and your memories. I knew it had to be difficult for him to unbury it, and even harder to share it with a stranger.

His plan worked. After a while my breathing slowed, and with that the pain became much less intense. By the time his story ended, I was feeling comfortable enough to try to stand. I slowly got to my feet, took a few tentative steps, and was relieved to find only a dull ache in my side. But when I turned around to thank Tito for his kindness to me, he was already gone.

In just the past few weeks I'd been chased and threatened and arrested. I'd narrowly escaped a riot, a rumble, a shooting, and a good ol' South-of-the-Border knife fight. If these experiences accomplished anything, they served to ground me a bit. I no longer felt the need to search out trouble.

Besides, I think it had my number.

# 28

We got an unexpected phone call from Penelope. She had been contacted by a local television news station that was looking to interview some punk rockers... any punk rockers. She asked if we would be willing to be questioned at the Oxford House. After some discussion, we decided to go ahead with it. Not only would this be fun, but it would be an opportunity to present ourselves in a positive way, instead of as just another cliché of punk rock violence.

Six or seven of us were sitting patiently in our living room, waiting for these strangers to finish setting up. The reporter was a young guy, slender and well-dressed; he informed us that it would be a sort of free-for-all... he would ask general questions, and he encouraged any of us who had a response to just jump on in. He was friendly and upbeat, and I returned his smile. This was going to be great. Finally, they were ready; the reporter took a seat across from us, and it began.

He started by asking us about our clothes and hair and music, then later moved on to our goals in life, and our relationships with our parents. Most of the kids were estranged from their folks and said little in response to that question, so I spoke up to describe the closeness my family shared.

After about half an hour more the interview began to wind down. The reporter finished by asking us where we expected to be in ten years. We looked at each other blankly. Ten *years*? We rarely looked ahead ten days... To break the silence, I chirped up and announced that I would probably be married and have a dozen kids, as long as I always got to have adventures. He seemed to like that answer. The interview ended, and he thanked us for our time.

Man, I couldn't wait for it to appear! It was scheduled for the following night, so we all made sure to be home for the six o'clock news. The national stories were at the top of the broadcast, followed by a discussion of a local event, and then another local event... and then, there we were!

It was odd. The original interview took nearly an hour, yet our segment was condensed to not more than a minute. Perhaps that was just as well... seeing as we ended up sounding like every other interview made punks sound.

Like a bunch of idiots.

It was sixty seconds of off-the-cuff jokes and teasing and the occasional rowdy aside. Any response we had made that sounded even remotely negative was in, while those discussions that displayed wit and insight disappeared. My comment about my parents was one of those that ended up on the cutting room floor.

The segment ended with my declaration about adventures. With that the camera returned to the co-anchors, where it caught the appalled newswoman shaking her head in disgust. The sentiment was silently returned.

We had one more unpleasant encounter with the press, but this time it took a different form.

Maggie had been offered a chance to be on a talk show - just like Dick Cavett's! Okay, not exactly Dick Cavett... after all, it was just a local station... but it was still a talk show! They said that they wanted to speak to a real punk rocker, get her views on life and music and stuff. At first Maggie didn't want to do it, but we figured that this time it wouldn't be some cut-and-spliced interview. This time she could say whatever she wanted.

After a bit more coaxing, she acquiesced. On the day of the taping Maggie was cool - almost blasé - but not me! I was bursting with excitement for her!

The TC were sitting in front of the television set, waiting for Maggie's debut. I had never seen this particular show, and was unfamiliar with the show's host. Apparently he had at one time been some kind of minor celebrity, but those days were long gone. The man was Pure Wesson, from his polished shoes and leisure slacks, to the gold chain draped around his neck.

Maggie sat alone on the small, white stage, and listened in disbelief to his questions... he didn't even bother to conceal his contempt for her. What did you do to your hair? How do you get a comb through it? Who buys your clothes? Confused at first, she nevertheless held her own, and answered him roundly, but politely. He clearly wasn't getting what he wanted from her - so he switched to a different tack.

What about her parents? Was she close to them? And her mother? Did she see her mother often? Maggie mumbled something and shifted in her chair; she was visibly uncomfortable with this new line of questioning.

The host leaned forward. "Well, why don't we ask her?" He looked up and raised his voice. "Mrs. ___, is that you?"

"Yes." It was Maggie's mother, speaking on her kitchen telephone; she sounded baffled, and more than a little annoyed.

Maggie had been set up.

"What is your relationship with your daughter? Do you see her often?" At that, the camera came in for a close-up on Maggie's face. Her mother's voice echoed throughout the studio.

"Well... she usually comes over when she needs something." For Christ's sake.

The audience snickered derisively - and Maggie laughed with them. She wasn't about to give them the satisfaction of anything else.

Not long after, the interview came to a merciful close. It was the last one any of us would do.

# 29

As the days went, by a general feeling of unease grew between us; we were now more like mistrustful inmates than a tight-knit family. We still went to gigs together, but they reflected the changes in our house. One venue especially, the Cuckoo's Nest in Costa Mesa, illustrated the increasing violence and lack of punk unity.

In Los Angeles, punk rock had been born in the streets of Hollywood. While clearly influenced by their brethren in England and New York, bands like X and the Germs found their own voice and style; X mixed punk with rockabilly, while the Germs took the anything-goes antics of The Stooges, and raised it to a new level of guttural expression and self-destruction. After a few years, however, Hollywood punk was submerged by the increasingly aggressive style of the beach punks.

Punk rock had tapped a nerve in the beach communities; the kids showing up now were even younger, tougher, and more physical. The problem, however, was not in the age, or the strength, of this new kind of punk; it came down to sheer numbers. The scene was exploding, and with it came kids who were there less for the music than they were for the opportunity to hurt someone. Already brimming with frustration or anger, it was easy for them to use the pit as a way to strike out, and still hide under the pretense of 'just slamming'.

On this particular night, I followed Black Flag down to the Cuckoo's Nest. As the band assembled backstage, I walked across the floor, getting the feel of the place. Though early, it was already packed; the room stank of sweat, and stale beer. There was not one familiar face.

When the opening chords of Six Pack rang out, the pit erupted in a blur of violent motion. There must have been a couple of hundred boys, and none of them cared one wit that there was a girl down there amongst them. They hurled themselves around with a bruising force, and a hostility to match. It was then that I felt something that I had never experienced before in the pit.

I think it was fear.

Pushing my way through, I spent the rest of the night dancing by myself, well away from the mob.

It wasn't any better back at the house. Ricky and Brian had been spending more time together, and judging from their secretive whispers, it was likely that the trouble they had no doubt found was of an illegal nature. My suspicion was confirmed when I overheard a conversation that I was not meant to hear.

Later that evening, I awoke groggily to find Ricky and Brian standing over me. My attic bedroom was dark, and more than ever I felt its isolation. Ricky told me he had heard a rumor in the house that I was going to tell the police what they had done. He wanted to know if that was true. I glanced from Ricky to Brian, then back to Ricky. There was a kind of sizzling, threatening energy behind his eyes.

After being assured that the rumor was false, Ricky appeared to be satisfied, and he went back downstairs with Brian. Alone in the dark once again, I wondered whether they had come to my room to get information, or deliver a warning.

A couple of weeks later, Ricky stole from the house. It was minor stuff, really, but that didn't matter. For some strange reason, stealing from strangers was okay, but stealing from friends would not be tolerated. It was some kind of thieves' code, or something.

He was ambushed when he arrived home, and justice was meted out with fists behind a locked door.

Life at Oxford House was spiraling out of control.

# 30

Mark and Emil rarely skated with me anymore. Black Flag had recruited Emil as their new drummer, and as the band was notorious for their work ethic, Emil's days of leisure had been seriously curtailed. As far as Mark went, his days were taken up by his new girlfriend. Charlene was wide-eyed and lovely, with dark wavy hair and a classic complexion. I tried as hard as I could to dislike her.

There was a concert being held in the downtown area. I went with Mark and Charlene; she occupied the front seat, and I sat in the back. Mark kept one hand on the steering wheel, while his other hand intertwined her fingers in his own. Mark gazed at Charlene, Charlene gazed at Mark, and I wondered sourly if we would make it to the gig in one piece. At one point the car hit a pothole, making Charlene bump her head gently on the soft headrest. She cried out in surprise, and Mark comforted her right away. I rolled my eyes, and was relieved to finally arrive.

The hall was big, but there weren't many kids there. Between sets, Mark sat with Charlene on the edge of the stage; their heads were low, and they shared murmured thoughts, and the occasional kiss. I walked away, annoyed; this night was off to a bad start. It was about to get worse.

Anticipating the possibility of violence, the club's manager had hired some bouncers for the night's festivities. They were the typical large, thick-necked young men. There had been reports over the past few weeks of some of them taking their energy out on hapless lone punks who, intentionally or not, brought about their ire. With the single exception of the bouncer at the Vex, whose body I had used as a shield, I tried to avoid them.

A scuffle broke out on the floor. Three of the bouncers were kneeling on the hard surface, and they appeared to be beating up a young kid. Instinctively I ran up to the one on top and pulled his hair, in the hopes it would get his attention and stop him from hurting the kid any further. It got his attention, all right - the result of which was a large bicep placed in a chokehold around my neck.

The bouncer stood me up and began to drag me towards the door. Images of a back-alley beating flashed through my mind. I grabbed the hard, muscled forearm and dug my nails into him. He stopped, tightened his hold, and purred a low warning into my ear to cease what I was doing. I let go.

We were walking faster now. The back exit loomed before me... and then we turned. We were going towards the entrance. Punks jumped out of his way, as he shoved me out the door. I slipped on the pavement and went down. Without a word, he turned and went back into the hall.

I brushed off the tiny pebbles that had stuck to my palms when I fell; other than a scrape on my elbow and a couple of rips in my jeans, I was unhurt. There was another problem, however; I didn't have a dollar bill on me, and with no other way to get back inside, it looked like I'd be stuck there until the gig ended. The street was deserted now; it was primarily made up of warehouses, and shuttered ones at that. Great. Just great.

I was about to do some exploring when a figure emerged from the front entrance. It was Mark. He glanced around, and upon spotting me, trotted over.

"Are you all right?" His voice sounded worried. Then it hit me. He *was* worried. About me! He had seen me being dragged out by the bouncer, and *he was worried!* It gave me the most wonderful, bubbly feeling in my stomach.

As I opened my mouth to respond, there was another flurry of motion, and Charlene came breathlessly up to us. Damn. I eyed her resentfully as she echoed Mark's question. Smiling tightly, I assured her I was fine, and she sighed in relief.

"Thank goodness. I told Mark to go out and find you. I'm so glad you're okay."

The smile remained on my face, but I'm not sure how. 'I told Mark to go out - *I* told...' It was her idea to look for me - not Mark's.

It was a double humiliation; not only had Mark been indifferent to my welfare, but now I had to thank Charlene for her concern. I needn't have worried, though; by then she had grabbed his hand, he responded by pulling Charlene closer to him, and they walked off together, my presence all but forgotten. For one brief, glorious moment, I had allowed myself to hope. I would not make that mistake again.

Bobbi gave me a ride home after the show had ended. Her car had barely pulled away from the curb when I began to cry. She was clearly startled, and when she asked me what was wrong, my feelings about Mark came rushing out. I told her everything, everything that I had tried so hard to hide. By the time I got to this evening's fiasco, my sobs were taking on the form of hyperventilation.

"I don't get it! What's wrong with me, Bobbi? I'm not beautiful, like you and Maggie, but I'm not..." A thought suddenly occurred to me.

"Do I smell? Is that it?"

I grabbed the front of my shirt and inhaled deeply. There didn't appear to be anything unusually repugnant. I took a couple of more little sniffs, then sank dejectedly back into the ripped upholstery.

"What is wrong with me!" I wailed. Bobbi began to speak but then stopped, and her counsel was replaced by a sigh. I looked away, out the window, thoroughly demoralized, and miserable.

Bobbi let me out at the curb in front of the house. Leslie was there, sitting on the front porch; she had a nose for people who needed a good cry, and a shoulder to match. She listened to my sorry story, and after a brief pause, asked what Bobbi had said to me.

"What? I don't... she didn't say anything... I don't think." There was another silence after that, long enough for me to take notice.

"Why? What did you think she would say?"

"Well, I don't know, but..." Leslie was hesitating, and it was confusing me.

What was going on here?

Leslie finally turned and looked at me directly. "Bobbi told me she has a crush on you. She didn't want to say anything to you because you're straight."

I shook my head. A crush? How could Bobbi have a crush on me? She wasn't... I mean, she didn't... she had a boyfriend!

Leslie smiled, patted my knee sympathetically, and went back inside. I remained on the porch, as both the warm spring wind, and Leslie's words, dried my tears.

# 31

During the past couple of weeks Maggie had been hanging out more with Rachel, and leaving me behind. I didn't know what was causing the split. There was something going on, something that I didn't belong to, and couldn't identify. She would go in the kitchen with Rachel, and they would begin to whisper; sometimes a laugh would ring out, but without any hint of gaiety. Their growing friendship made me feel insecure, and unwanted, like I didn't fit in anymore. After a while I just tried to avoid them.

It wasn't just relationships that were falling apart. Even my hair started to dissolve. I had bleached it so much that all I had to do was touch it with my fingertips and it would break off in my hands. I went to the bathroom to try to fix it, but quickly changed my mind; two of the girls were already in there, shooting up drugs with water they sucked out of the toilet bowl.

I didn't know that much about drugs, as my college experience was limited to pot and hash, and occasionally cocaine. Heroin had been the popular drug on the punk scene, and it took its share of victims. But now there was a new word being heard more and more in our community: loads.

Loads meant a combination of different drugs, and it was messing people up bad. There was a girl named Christy who was a friend of both the TC and Bobbi, and she had just died of it; rumor had it that she had been in a room full of people, but everyone there was too stoned to help her, or even notice her distress. Christy was sweet and kind-hearted, and her death hit Bobbi hard.

The less time I spent with the TC, the closer I had become with Bobbi. Shortly after Christy's death, we drove up to the hills above Hollywood; they were a blessing, an oasis of trees and grass that made the sprawling metropolis seem far away. If any place could exorcise the demons of the city, this was it. We found a flat spot beside a tree and sat with our backs against it.

Bobbi looked so different from the first night I saw her. She had tempered the rage that had led her to burn that girl's hair; she found outlets for her anger now, and it no longer ruled her. While she never talked to me about her days on the streets prior to my meeting her, I did know that her life up until then had been a rough one. But instead of finding solace in drugs as so many did, Bobbi took her experiences and her memories and turned to writing. She started a band called Red Scare, becoming both the singer and songwriter. It was truly astonishing to hear such a powerful voice come out of a person as little as she was. Even in a rehearsal room cramped with mikes and speakers and boxes, all eyes were on her.

Bobbi gazed across the hill, a half-smile on her face. She was a firecracker, to be sure, but at the same time she had a calmness about her, as if she had learned all the answers to all her questions, long ago. It was a quality I would come to envy in the weeks ahead.

# 32

While I stayed well away from drugs, they did play a part in a strange reunion.

I was at the house, alone; everyone else had left earlier for a gig at the Whiskey. It was late, almost midnight, when boots scuffed along the front porch and the front door banged open. It was Rachel, but she wasn't alone; she was lugging someone inside with her. The stranger was alarmingly thin, with greasy black hair that stood out sharply against his sallow skin. She brought him over to the couch and dumped him there with an impatient gasp. I crossed the room and looked down at him.

It was Johnny Thunders.

Rachel told me that she had met Johnny at the Whiskey and hooked up with him. It wasn't long before he passed out, however, and she found herself stuck with an incoherent doper. Bringing him here seemed to be her best option.

She moved towards the door, and it was then that I realized she was leaving him here - with me.

"Rachel, wait! What about him? I mean - well, is he all right?"

A quick glance. "He'll be okay."

I shook my head, unconvinced. "But..."

"He'll be *okay*," she repeated confidently. "Don't worry." With that she shut the door firmly behind her; her light step retreated down the pavement.

I looked over at Johnny uneasily; whatever drugs he was on, he was certainly out of it. He seemed to be asleep, or maybe even unconscious; every once in a while he would make this weird, deep gurgling sound. The wild figure that had once so thrilled me had rotted away, like a piece of wood abandoned to the elements. Whether it was due to alcohol or heroin or loads, he was being destroyed from the inside out. But as pathetic as it was, it didn't touch my awe of him. He was still Johnny Thunders.

I lay down on the floor next to the couch. An hour must have passed, as my ears strained for the least little sound that would indicate he was in real trouble. After a while, though, his breathing became more easy and regular. Rachel had been right, after all.

The next morning I was sitting at the bottom of the stairs, playing with some kittens we had recently found. It was early still, and after their late night, everyone else was asleep. I looked up to find Johnny watching me, his eyes amused and friendly. The old shyness enveloped me once again; I didn't know what to say to him.

"I saw you in 1977 at the Village Gate," I finally blurted out.

Johnny's expression changed with that; it was still warm, but there was a sadness now that had been absent before.

"That was a long time ago," he responded quietly. Then he left. I never saw him again.

Years later, I read of Johnny Thunders' death. He died of a drug overdose.

# 33

For a while after the incident with the reporter, things had been fairly frosty at the office. Biggs no longer trusted me, and I had lost faith in him. But at least there were no more blow-ups, and Slash was able to offer me a needed escape from the Oxford House.

Earlier in the year X's first record had received critical acclaim, even being named Best Album by the Los Angeles Times. As the release of their new album grew closer, there was again an undercurrent of excitement. Press releases had to be written, posters had to be designed, and the band continued to silently tromp past me on their way into Biggs' office. Life at Slash was back to normal.

Biggs walked into the office during this time and handed me an unnerving assignment. The new album was to be called Wild Gift, and Biggs needed the master brought over to the engineer. If that happened today, a bonded courier would no doubt be used - but in 1981, it was all up to me.

I placed the tapes in the seat beside me, and pulled out into traffic. The engineer's studio was only a few miles away, but the possibilities of disaster sprung up before me. What if I dropped them? What if I ruined them? What if... what if... what if X had to *re-record* them?!

The little car resonated with a kind of mantra... "Just don't crash." "Just don't crash..." "JUST DON'T CRASH!" Considering that I wasn't even a Buddhist, the chant was actually fairly successful. Cars stopped at stop signs, no one ran a red light... in general, the universe decided to behave itself. It was only after the tapes were in the arms of the waiting engineer, however, that I allowed myself to relax. A priceless Ming vase could not have formented more sheer terror than those simple metal canisters of reel.

I still checked out gigs, but more and more I did so on my own.

There was a kid who sometimes hung around the clubs. He had been showcased in Penelope's movie as an 'example' of how a punk rocker acted and spoke, but I think she put him in there primarily because he said so many stupid things. His name was Mike, and he was the son of a cop, but he was known on the streets as 'X-Head'.

X-Head had achieved his moniker by shaving a giant 'X' into his dark hair. Though short in stature, he was infamous for his cowardly enjoyment of picking fights. In conjunction with cruel, squinty eyes, he sported a perpetual grin which nevertheless managed to belie any trace of wit.

On this particular night he introduced himself to me, so to speak, outside the Starwood. It was late, and because I was alone, my isolation had made me vulnerable; X-Head honed in on that like a shark to chum.

"Hey, bitch." No response. "Yeah you, bitch, I'm talking to you."

Oh! That would be me! I waited, but he didn't say anything after that. Was this some punk rock version of a courting ritual? If so, I figured I'd pass; after all, 'hey you bitch' wasn't exactly a pink corsage pinned to my blouse.

He took a step closer. And then there it was. The grin. The one I had heard so much about. The one that said he wanted to fight me.

I mulled that over in my brain for a moment. He actually wanted to fight me. He wanted to fight *me*. I guess I should have been scared, and I was for a minute, but then... I don't know. The whole thing suddenly seemed so... well, ludicrous. That's when I started to giggle.

Clearly this was not the response he anticipated. X-Head's face, already pale under the harsh street lamp, grew even whiter. It probably wasn't very smart to react to him this way, but I couldn't help it. Tears came to my eyes, and I didn't even bother to brush them away.

His mouth tightened into a hard straight line, but curiously enough, X-Head didn't strike out at me. He thought about it, but his pattern of intimidation and attack had been disrupted. After a moment of hesitation, he split - in search of fresher and more cooperative prey, I suppose.

The laughter left me then, as quickly as it had begun; my legs gave out, and I sat down on the pavement beneath me.

It's funny... The laughter was gone. But the tears still fell.

# 34

The summer that brought so much change had come to an end, and I wanted to leave.

I had had enough of the grim life at Oxford House and the growing violence at the shows. The uniqueness and joy that the scene once held for me had slowly disintegrated, leaving in its place monotony, and conformity, and an overall, depressing gloom. I had to get out of there.

Returning east to my parents' house, I obtained a passport and made plans to travel through Europe by rail. Exploring on my own proved to be as exciting as anticipated; despite the pleasure of these new experiences, however, Los Angeles kept pushing itself back into my mind, like a haunting memory - or maybe just a haunting.

Early on in my trip, a young couple shared my train compartment while we journeyed to the north of England. As we exchanged stories and backgrounds, the woman revealed that she was a teacher at an elementary school. But not just any school.

She taught at the elementary school that backed up against the St. Andrews house.

A couple of weeks later I sat on a dock in Venice, my legs swinging freely over the side. Gazing across at the rows of laundry-draped balconies, I wondered what Maggie and Emil and

Bobbi were doing. Were they at a gig right now? Maybe they were skating some rad pool, or getting into a rumble, or... I returned to the hostel to discover that a letter had been forwarded to me by my parents. It was from Malissa! I tore it open, the pages tumbling haphazardly onto the bed. The envelope contained gold: sheet after sheet of updates on the TC.

It seemed that the Oxford House was no more; apparently, they had neglected to pay the rent for two months, and had lost their lease. The Oziehares were still playing the occasional show, and Maggie had started a new band with Emil and Pat Smear called Twisted Roots. They were slated to open at the Whiskey in just a few weeks.

Strangely enough, the further I had travelled from Los Angeles, the more I found I missed it. With each passing day the old stings - once so painful - had lessoned in degree, until their hurt had completely faded away. By the time my decision was made, it wasn't even a surprise. Nostalgia, or need, had replaced intuition. I was going back.

I called Maggie with the news, and we agreed to become roommates again. I couldn't wait to return! As my plane took me back to the West Coast, however, the flight was tainted by a nagging uneasiness. I loved Maggie dearly, but *something* had happened to our friendship at the Oxford House. In Europe, it was easy to assign it labels: one day it was just my own paranoia, or the natural, childlike jealousy of seeing a best friend spending time with someone else. Other days her coldness was blamed on drug use of some kind. The truth was, it couldn't be explained... but a mistrust had formed between us. It was vague, and undefined, but it was there; it poisoned looks and words, and even laughter.

The uncertainty I was feeling vanished when Maggie picked me up at the airport. It was great to see her again, and the drive into Hollywood was filled with easy and lighthearted gossip. I had my best friend back.

Maggie was living in a pretty two-bedroom apartment on Genesee, and she gave me the spare bedroom. It felt a little strange to be living again in such a conventional way, but that was soon forgotten in the fun of buying bedspreads and rugs and pictures, and even pots and pans.

The next thing up was to find work. My first thought was of Slash. Despite quitting weeks earlier, I was hoping there might still be a place for me. After all, there were no hard feelings - Biggs had wished me the best of luck in whatever I did, and I could tell he was sincere. I climbed the stairs as I had so many times before, and rounded the bend. There was a girl in the reception room - and she was sitting in my chair. All right, I know it wasn't *exactly* my chair, but before I came they didn't even have a chair, and now a stranger was in it. My chair, I mean. She was young and pretty and cheerful, and... normal. Really, really normal. It just didn't look right.

Biggs greeted me in a friendly manner, and listened with understanding to my request for a job. And turned me down. The job had been filled. Period. Oh, and one more thing. Best of luck. He wished me the best of luck. Once misinterpreted as warm regards, the phrase now had the distinct ring of finality.

As I walked past my replacement, she smiled at me awkwardly. I went down Slash's staircase, for the last time.

Next up was the want ads. I didn't know what job was right for me, so I took the first one I could find - making telephone sales pitches. Later came temporary work at a book company, answering phones. During this time Twisted Roots had pressed their first single, and the band was preparing for their approaching gig at the Whiskey. Our positions were now reversed; Maggie had finally found something to throw all her energy into, while I had no idea what I wanted. There was my degree, of course. And I did check under the C's in the want ads. There were no openings for a cultural anthropologist.

Around this time Maggie and I decided to throw our first real, grown-up dinner party. The entree would be spaghetti. Maggie would make her special, takes-all-day-to-cook, pasta sauce.

The guests would be Black Flag.

As we didn't have a dining table yet, or even any chairs, the members of the band sat on the floor. By that time I had come to know both Chuck and Greg, but their new singer, Henry, was an enigma. He was intimidating, to be sure, with muscular, tatooed arms, and dark eyes that seemed to pierce your soul with a glance. I was a little afraid of him; I'm sure I didn't know how to approach him, and the dinner party did nothing to clarify his personality. On the other hand, maybe it did. He came, he ate, he left - and never said one word.

If Maggie felt the slight, she didn't show it, but Henry sure got me mad; after working on her sauce all day, the least he should have done was thank her. But I let it go. Sometimes I wonder what the Black Flag singer's reaction would have been, to find himself chastised for poor dinner manners...

"Amie, you have the longest lashes I've ever seen."

Startled, I peered across the dark room. The statement had come from one of the boys, and it left me completely disconcerted. Snubs and slights from a guy was one thing; I was used to that. But compliments? I had just put a forkful of spaghetti in my mouth, and I swallowed the hunk of pasta, hard. A response was clearly expected, but my mind had gone blank. They were waiting.

"When God made me, he said I could pick one thing, so I chose long eyelashes."

What? What did I just say?

There were baffled glances from across the room.

Oh, please, tell me I didn't say that. Not *out loud!* I tried mumbling 'thank you', but by then it was too late. I knew where the quote came from - it was from another S. E. Hinton book. Maybe if I explained...

"'Tex'... the book 'Tex', I mean - it's from this book, you see"... My voice trailed off. The band was discussing their next concert.

Our first dinner party soon came to a close, to my great relief. Looking back, perhaps I would have appreciated it more - had I known it was to be our last.

# 35

Maggie and I were on our way to a party in the Valley. Actually, we were on our way to crash a party in the Valley, since we didn't know the kids who threw it. Even with an address and a map, we got lost twice just trying to find their house.

When we got there we could hear the sound of a bass from inside, along with shouts and glass breaking. The party had obviously been in full swing for some time, as already there was a party-goer throwing up on the immaculate lawn.

This was different than the usual Hollywood parties, or even the ones held down in Huntington Beach. Not a soul here was recognizable, and the band was bad; playing a Valley party was probably going to be the highlight of their short career. And while the kids there were dressed like punks, I got the impression that this was something they didn't do very often. As enticing as the thought of leaving was, it just wasn't an option. After all, it took us a hell of a long time just to find the place. We weren't going anywhere.

Sometime during the evening, Maggie and I became separated. Wandering around on my own, I was startled to hear Maggie's voice rise above the din.

"Get off of me. Get the *fuck* off of me!" She didn't sound angry. She sounded scared.

I pushed my way through the crowd and found her; she was

on her back, and a young man was trying to pin her down. I ran to him, grabbed hold of his hair, and pulled; he yelped and let go, giving Maggie the chance to slip from his grasp.

I wasn't so lucky. His girlfriend, enraged by my interference, came to his defense. She was a tough-looking girl, with black leather spiked bracelets wrapped around her wrists. I didn't even get a word out. She decked me.

It all happened so fast I didn't even react. While my eyes screamed 'Fist incoming!', my brain responded dully 'Where?' as her knuckle clipped my eye. My hand went up belatedly, rubbing the sting at the top of my cheek. Slowly it dawned on me what had just happened, and I broke out in a wide smile.

I finally had my black eye.

My attacker was completely taken aback by my reaction; she was prepared for an angry, even violent response, not this daft girl grinning ear to ear. It was when I *thanked* her for hitting me, though, that she retreated back into the crowd. She had clearly had enough of me.

Where was Maggie? One girl told me she was outside, but another boy pointed upstairs to the master bathroom. He was sure he saw a girl with black dreadlocks head that way.

Upstairs, I tapped on the closed bathroom door, but there was no response. Behind me, two punk girls were arguing about who was the best band in Los Angeles. When one of the girls asserted that that title belonged to Black Flag, her companion snorted in derision. She began to rag on the band, attacking their songs and their lyrics and their singer... and then she bad-mouthed Emil.

Her companion returned to the party, but as the girl prepared to join her downstairs, I blocked her exit. I informed her that I was a friend of Black Flag. I was a friend of Emil. And then I threatened her... but when I did so, it wasn't as 'I'. It was 'we'. *We* were better than her. *We* wouldn't put up with her shit.

We could find out who she was.

You'd think she would have been afraid, but she wasn't. She

didn't apologize. She said nothing at all. She merely pushed past me, her shoulder banging mine in a sign of contempt. Standing in that room, I couldn't have felt any lower. I had tried to frighten a young girl... precisely for doing what I never did anymore. For speaking her mind. I caught a glimpse of my reflection in the mirror, and wondered who that was staring back at me.

I wanted to get out of there and forget what had happened. What I had done. Downstairs was even more crowded now, and Maggie was nowhere around. Someone grabbed my arm; it was the girl with the spiked bracelets. Oh great, now what? I'd had enough of her, her friends, this house, the party and the Valley. All I wanted to do was go home.

The music was deafening. She had to press her mouth against my ear to be heard.

"Where's your friend?" she demanded.

"My friend?... I don't know. Why?"

Her face grew ugly. "Why? Oh, okay, I'll tell you why - because she stabbed my boyfriend, that's why!"

I tried to shove her away from me, but this time she held her ground.

"You're lying..."

"That bitch stabbed my boyfriend - from behind! You tell her we're looking for her."

I kept shaking my head. No. *No.* It wasn't true.

"You just tell her that."

The music was making my head throb. She was still yelling at me, her mouth by my ear, but I wouldn't listen. I wouldn't. I wasn't going to listen.

But I did.

# 36

I had left Maggie at the house to wander around the neighborhood, and eventually stumbled upon a 7-11. The clock in the convenience store read 4 a.m. At that time of the morning the coffee was free; the black beverage in the styrofoam cup felt warm between my hands, but if I was expecting that to provide comfort, I was out of luck.

Even though I knew Maggie, saw examples of her innate decency every day... even though she was my best friend... I believed this stranger. Completely. Maybe it was the leftovers of mistrust spawned at the Oxford House that allowed me to accept the story so readily. Whatever it was, it had thrown my life into a tailspin.

'She stabbed him... ' The words themselves made me feel ill. They couldn't be ignored, nor could they be justified. This wasn't about stealing a copy machine anymore. I was drawing a moral line in the sand, today, right now, and I wasn't crossing it.

It was obvious what had to be done. I had to return to the party, confront Maggie, find out why she had done... what she had done. The day that Ricky was jumped at the Oxford House, I stood against the wall and did nothing to stop it. Not a damn thing. That wasn't going to happen this time. At least, that's what I told myself.

The problem was, speaking my mind required a courage that I did not yet have. It would mean facing the unhappiness and the pain that could hide behind a smile. It would mean standing up to Maggie and receiving her anger in return... or worse, her ridicule. Much easier to just pretend it didn't happen, right? So that's what I did.

It was easier, yes. But I couldn't escape the cost.

# 37

Did you ever walk on a sheet of ice, certain that it would hold your weight - then when you pressed down, really pressed down, it cracked? You could watch the angular lines forge across the surface, making figures of different sizes and shapes; even as it created its own kind of beauty, you knew the ice was weakened forever. You couldn't step on that sheet again - not unless you wanted to fall into the icy water underneath. I knew this.

But I had stepped onto the ice anyway.

As if by an unspoken pledge, Maggie and I both pretended that nothing extraordinary had occurred, and we did manage to continue an appearance of normalcy, at least for a while. Dishes were washed, beds were made, we shopped together and even made dinner together. Emil knew something was up, though I hadn't told him what happened. Perhaps Maggie had.

As expected, the skin around my eye swelled, and turned a striking shade of purple and black. My satisfaction was stolen, however, when neither Maggie nor Emil acknowledged it. It was nothing special. Just a black eye, with no history behind it...

One afternoon, Maggie came into my room. It sounded as if she was trying to explain the attack, but oddly enough it was her movements, and not her words, that drew my attention. As she spoke she backed further and further away from me, until her body was actually trapped between the door and the wall. Maggie had literally talked herself into a corner. In a strange, detached way, I found that interesting.

The bond and trust between us was deteriorating fast, and we knew it. I was still horrified by the stabbing - but if our friendship was going to survive, I had to make myself get past the numbness and uncertainty that had kept me silent, and talk to the girl...

It was a few days after the party, close to midnight. With barely a coherent thought in my head, I went to Maggie's room and knocked. Emil yelled for me to come on in.

My hand on the doorknob, I took a deep breath and entered. They were both laying in bed, under the covers, and in an embrace - not a good start, seeing that the situation was awkward enough as it was. I held my ground, and even took a couple of steps towards them. Almost on cue, they turned towards me, and my heart froze. Without another word I left the room.

It was the look on Maggie's face that sent me backwards through the doorway. She had worn that expression once before - but only once.

On the cover of a newspaper.


Morning came. My footsteps were light as they crossed the living room floor. All of a sudden gravity released me, and I rose into the air. It was a nice feeling, really... almost exhilarating - until I tried to get down. I couldn't. My arms bobbed helplessly by my sides, and my legs felt light and hollow. Maggie was there now. She was watching me, expressionless. I needed her help, but even as my mouth formed words, no sounds came out. I couldn't speak, I couldn't get down... I couldn't do anything. My body passed over Maggie's head, bumping along the ceiling, like a balloon...

I opened my eyes. The ceiling was where it belonged, several feet above me. Laying there quietly, I reassured myself that everything was okay - the dream was over. But when I reached up to touch my face, I found the remnants of tears. My finger slowly traced the damp, meandering path they had made down my cheek. And after a while, I knew. I knew that this had been more than a dream.

The ice had just shattered beneath me.

# 38

If asked today what it was like to be a punk rocker in the early eighties, I'd probably answer... that there is no one answer. How could there be? It's true that punks had superficial features in common, like clothes and hair - and later, we formed an even deeper bond with our shared experiences. But in the end, we really were all just small pieces of an incredible puzzle. That's why our stories are so varied, and contradictory, and unique.

For me, it came down to this... I had needed friends, and found them. I had sought out danger, even as it was erupting before me. I wanted to have fun - and being a punk rocker was surely that. But it took a long time for me to see - really see - so much of the ugliness around me: the drugs, the violence, the lack of trust, and the betrayal of trust. Looking back, it's hard to believe that the majority of events in this book happened in a span of only eighteen months.

As for my mistakes, there were plenty of those - and yet I doubt they could have been prevented. Naiveté is something that one just has to grow out of, while maturity and wisdom... well, I'm still working on that. We, each of us, have a struggle to undertake; mine was finding my own voice, and having the courage to stand by it. Maggie and Malissa and the rest of the TC made their journeys, as well - but in their own time, and in their own way.

So I finally got my adventure - because really, that's what it was. Not a lifestyle. Not a core being. It didn't define me. I could leave it behind, and move on to the next new and wonderful experience.

Some might argue that that made me a poser. I don't know... maybe it did.

But I could still slamdance with the best of them.

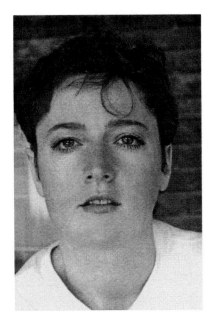

The author lives on her ranch in Texas.
This is her first book.